Constable Stephen Grant
of
The North-West Mounted Police

in

The Post Must Get Through

by
Andrew Ferns

Madeira Park, British Columbia, Canada

As always, for My Family…

The Post Must Get Through
Originally published by the author in 2025.

ISBN: 978-1-0694089-3-8

CONTENTS

CHAPTER		PAGE
I	A DANGEROUS MISSION	1
II	A CHANGE OF PLAN	7
III	THE PATH AHEAD	13
IV	THE REUNION	20
V	A ROUGH START	25
VI	THE CHILKOOT	30
VII	THE FIRST ATTEMPT	38
VIII	CRATER LAKE	47
IX	THE SUMMIT	53
X	A HARROWING DESCENT	60
XI	A TEMPORARY REFUGE	69
XII	A BLOWN COVER	75
XIII	RACING TO SKAGWAY	82
XIV	CONFRONTATION AT THE DOCKS	86
XV	GOD BLESS THE ROYAL NAVY	93
XVI	SAFE PASSAGE	102
XVII	SOAPY'S WRATH	108
XVIII	THE NEXT TASK	114
XIX	THE SECOND ATTEMPT	119
XX	THE CONFRONTATION	128
XXI	THE GROWING CONFLICT	134
XXII	ENTER GEORGE	143
XXIII	TAKING THE MAIL	148
XXIV	THE PERILS OF THE TRAIL	157
XXV	FULL CIRCLE	163
XXVI	FAREWELLS & DESCENTS	170
XXVII	THE RETURN TO BENNETT	174
XXVIII	JUNEAU WHARF	180

ABOUT THE AUTHOR

Andrew Ferns is a Canadian filmmaker, writer, and producer with a diverse career spanning film, television, and literature. A graduate of Dalhousie University and Mount Royal University, Andrew's work bridges both the creative and production sides of the industry, offering a unique perspective to his storytelling.

His documentary credits include award-winning projects such as *Captain Cook: Obsession and Discovery* and *Darwin's Brave New World*, both of which earned multiple accolades. He also produced the feature film *Painkillers*, which won the AMPIA Award for Best Dramatic Feature Film.

As a writer, Andrew's debut novel, the supernatural thriller *Disappear: Into Shadow* demonstrated his ability for crafting suspenseful, character-driven narratives. He has also created historical content, including the *Monumental Canadians* web series for Valour Canada, which received numerous accolades.

Beyond film and literature, Andrew has produced bespoke visual content for brands like Enbridge and the Calgary Stampede; and has worked with The Walt Disney Company, NBC Universal, and HBO overseeing Production Health and Safety on major titles like *Big Sky*, *The Fall Guy*, and *The Last of Us*.

In this latest book, Andrew continues to immerse readers in his world of intricate storytelling, where complex characters and high-stakes tension collide. He resides on the Sunshine Coast of British Columbia, Canada, with his wife, where the landscapes and the land's rich history continue to inspire his creative work.

OTHER WORKS BY THE AUTHOR:

Disappear: Into Shadow ISBN: 978-1069408921

The Dead Horse Trail ISBN: 979-8311275118

THE POST MUST GET THROUGH

The Grant Chronicles

Book II

CHAPTER I

A Dangerous Mission

The early spring of 1898 brought the gentle warming of the frontier, a slow thawing of the snows that had blanketed the peaks and forests of the Klondike through the long winter. The creeping return to warmth carried with it the promise of change and of peril. Under the pressure of this change, the transition of the ice-covered lakes and rivers from their once-impenetrable surfaces began with cracks and groans, like the arthritic joints of a giant waking from a long, deep slumber.

When the spring's breakup arrived, it came sudden and violent. The massive sheets of ice that had been locked in place all winter shifted and broke apart with thunderous cracks. The deep sounds reverberated across the entire valley, as though the earth itself was shaking off the heavy burden of winter. When the chunks of ice, some the size of cabins, started to move they bumped and ground against one another, breaking off into jagged fragments as they drifted across the lakes toward the moving waters of the rivers that lead into the Yukon.

Previously a solid highway for dragging sleds and towing boats, the ice became treacherous and unstable. Anyone traveling on or near it had to move with extreme caution. The shifting ice caused sudden and dangerous changes in water levels. Those caught unprepared often found themselves stranded or even in perilous danger as the rivers swelled.

The once immobile, frozen paths of white became alive with motion and chaos. The icebergs that broke free into the rivers were carried by strong currents, creating jagged ice floes that collided and against each other with tremendous force.

Caroming downstream against the thick blued ice that still clung to the shorelines high above the riverbanks, the ice churned and split. Vast, chaotic jumbles of broken shards transformed the rivers into turbulent masses of floating debris. The spectacle of nature's raw power and beauty was an incredible reminder of the force of the water that had been forgotten beneath the ice.

As the ice broke up, the methodical, cold river currents began to flow freely. The water levels swelled and flooded to reclaim their former territories. The higher banks, which had been hidden under snowdrifts for months, appeared again, muddy and sometimes treacherous with the thawing frost.

For the trappers and Stampeders living in the tented encampments around Bennett Lake, spring breakup marked the beginning of a busy new season. The completion of their boats for the downstream journey to Dawson City reached a fevered pitch. Hammers and saws could be heard working through the night with little break in their choruses. The rush to finish building the rudimentary boats, to load their supplies, and ensure their equipment was ready became a frantic race to be ready at the first moment the river conditions allowed travel. The final leg of the marathon to reach the goldfields was approaching rapidly.

It was not just a time of celebration, but another reminder of the Klondike's unforgiving nature, and the breakup of the rivers was both a blessing and a danger to all who had called it home over the last months of winter.

Here, far from the comforts of civilization found in the continent's southern cities, across these remote regions, the North-West Mounted Police were hard at work. The rugged terrain, the continual threat of outlaws, and the unforgiving elements were all part of their daily existence.

The sound of knee-high, hard-heeled leather riding boots echoed across the wooden floors of the barracks at Bennett Lake. In the early hours of morning, before the sun had broken the edge of the horizon, the light from an oil lamp flickered softly from the small office at the rear of the building. While one shift of the detachment's Constables was wrapped in their brief cocoons of sleep, Superintendent Sam Steele sat inside a small office. His broad, stoic figure cast a shadow over the desk before him. He was surrounded by maps, letters and various official documents and registers. He was a towering figure, built like a bear with a military precision in his posture. Steele's reputation preceded him, his work with the NWMP was already regarded as legendary, but today there was a noticeable tension about him, the kind that came with a mission of great importance.

In his hand was a letter, the edges creased from the hurried way it had been passed along the frontier's often broken chain of communication. When he heard the knock at the office door, he held it for a moment longer, as if weighing its contents, before folding it neatly and placing it on the desk.

"Come," he beckoned.

His gaze then shifted towards the man who entered, Inspector Zachary Taylor Wood.

Wood was a man of method and precision, known for his cool head and sharp instincts. They had served together for years now. Wood had weathered storms before, both literal and figurative, but this mission would be unlike any he had faced before. Wood's uniform was impeccably neat. The red serge of his jacket, the gleaming brass buttons and polished black riding boots demonstrated the man's pride and authority. The distinctive wide brimmed Biltmore Stetson was set firmly on his head, and his close shorn blonde hair was, Steele had little doubt, well-groomed underneath.

Steele watched Wood take a steady breath as he squared his shoulders to attention. He knew this next assignment was going to test everything Wood had ever learned as a Mountie.

"Inspector Wood," Steele said, his voice steady and unflinching. "You have fresh orders. I must warn you; this mission will not be without its dangers. Significant dangers"

Wood nodded, his lips pressing into a thin line. When Sam Steele called, you answered no matter the task. He held no illusions that anything in this frontier was ever easy.

Steele handed Wood the creased letter, "As you'll read, the customs duties and other monies collected across the Territory has become a very large sum. We cannot afford to keep it in the Klondike any longer. It needs to be transported out and taken down to Victoria. I've chosen you to lead this mission."

"Sir," Wood replied.

"This isn't any ordinary shipment of gold and money you'll be moving," Steele said, and chose his next words carefully. "This money represents our authority in the region. Inevitably, we have no other option than to pass through Skagway."

Wood scanned the contents of the letter, a sense of gravity building within him. Skagway, known for its lawlessness and its notoriety as a haven for criminality, was a place few trusted. Soapy Smith, a man whose criminal empire was as vast as it was ruthless, controlled that town with an iron fist. Wood had heard the rumours and stories of men who disappeared in Skagway, never to be seen again. To pass through there with a large sum of money was to enter the belly of the beast and tempt its hunger with another succulent meal.

He was a steady man of firm resolve, and Wood set his jaw, before answering, "I understand Soapy Smith's operations in Skagway are notorious. You can't even walk down the street without feeling his presence. We'll be walking right into his domain, sir."

"That's correct," Steele replied. "You heard about the incident at White Pass, yes?" Seeing Wood nod his head, the Superintendent continued, saying, "Smith has already made one attempt to steal these duties. While that attempt did fail, it was a near run thing. We cannot allow him to make another brazen attempt." He pointed towards the map posted on the wall beside the desk, "Taking an overland route east was suggested to me, to avoid the issue. However, it will be too slow, requiring too many resources travelling away from the Territory for too long." The Superintendent shook his head, "No, it must be escorted out over the mountains to Skagway and then passaged by ship on to Vancouver Island."

Wood turned his gaze toward the window beside the map. The pale blue light of dawn was beginning to colour the mountains in the distance. The encampment at Bennett Lake was an isolated haven for the Mounties, and he could hear the world's ceaseless preparations for their next steps towards Dawson City. The wilderness, framed by jagged snow-covered mountains looked serene from the window, but Wood knew how quickly things could change. Beneath that beauty lay the real danger of the Klondike: unpredictable weather, treacherous terrain, and the greed of men like Soapy Smith.

"I've been briefed on Smith's men," Wood said. "We'll have to be cautious. His network runs deep, and they'll be looking for any sign of weakness and will seize any opportunity they can."

Steele replied, "Smith's gang is like a rotting tooth we haven't been able to pull, yet. You've gone up against his kind before. That's why I've chosen you for this task, Inspector."

"Thank you, Superintendent," Wood said, and stood ramrod straight as he prepared to take on the heavy responsibility. His mind already churned with strategies, contingencies, and the many dangers that lay ahead.

The mission was simple in its directive: get the money and gold to Victoria. But the route? It was fraught with obstacles. Harsh weather, treacherous trails, and the looming shadow of Soapy Smith's gang made this far more than just a set of mere logistical hurdles. The fate of the cargo, and perhaps even the law in this wild frontier now rested on the success of this mission.

Steele gave a tight nod and said, "I've sent word to Inspector Strickland at White Pass. He'll be sending down a Constable who has direct experience with this gang to assist you."

"I have my core team ready to go," Wood protested.

"Many hands make light work," Steele fired back. "This is not a request, Wood."

"Understood, sir."

"Keep your wits about you Zachary," Steele said as he leant back in his chair. He rubbed a hand along his jaw as he gave Wood a long, hard stare, "I trust you'll take every precaution. Don't disappoint me."

As Wood left the crudely hewn log barracks, the crisp air bit at his face. His mind was already focused on the mission ahead, and his heart raced. He had led men before, but this was different. Every step would be fraught with danger.

As he made his way from the barracks past the stables, Wood's mind considered the possibilities. He knew the journey to the coast would be long, and the terrain would test him beyond his limits. It was the threat of Soapy Smith's criminal network that worried him most. The man was a master manipulator whose organized syndicate openly controlled Skagway without remorse. No doubt Smith had eyes everywhere: on the docks, in the saloons, and perhaps even on this side of the border, along the very trails the Mounties would travel.

The stables, a crude wooden structure, were already bustling with Constables amid their morning routines, tending to their horses, adjusting their saddles, and checking their rifles. There was a rigid discipline to their movements, born of the constant need for vigilance in the wilderness. A couple of the Constables greeted him as he passed. Wood, however, had no time for small talk or leisurely preparation. He had received his orders.

The thawing ground beneath his boots squelched loudly as he walked through the massed tents of the camp and its maze of supply caches. When he reached one of the many makeshift boatyards, the sounds of axes and saws echoed through the cold air as men worked on the wooden hulls of boats meant for crossing treacherous stretches of lake and river.

Amongst this hive of activity, people worked tirelessly to build their boats and sledges, Wood inhaled the faint scent of spruce and pine resin and the raw tang of cold steel hanging in the air. He stared out across Bennett Lake, watching as the blue waters lapped at the ice-fringed shoreline. The landscape was both beautiful and inhospitable, a reminder of the power and indifference of nature itself.

Wood believed he was ready to face whatever awaited him. Over a decade of service in the Mounties had prepared him for any eventuality, but he could not help but feel this mission was going to be something entirely different. He knew he would not only be carrying money and gold, but the reputation of the North-West Mounted Police. He wasn't about to let Soapy Smith or anyone else tarnish it. With that thought, he felt the familiar sense of duty settle over him. That was a certainty he could keep his focus on.

CHAPTER II

A Change of Plan

Inside the log cabin at White Pass, Inspector D'Arcy Strickland sat behind his cluttered desk. His face was furrowed in concentration. The walls of the cabin were adorned with maps and charts, evidence of the chaotic military and logistical efforts that went into maintaining order along the rugged frontier border. His fingers drummed absently on the wood, a rhythm that matched the way his mind seemed to work as it constantly shifted between duties, decisions, and tactics. His prodigious black moustache twitched as he murmured soundless words to himself. The wood stove's fire crackled in the corner, but the heat did little to ease the cold edge of the task ahead.

Outside the cabin, the White Pass remained encased in snow and ice, the spring thaw had not yet begun to work its way up into the mountain passes. The air was sharp, and the landscape felt as though it remained frozen in time, like an unyielding sculpture carved by months of brutal winter. The Constables stationed at the Pass moved with a sense of purpose, as they were putting the finishing touches on the rebuild of their storehouse that had been destroyed in an attack by Soapy Smith's outlaws some months back.

Meanwhile, throughout the Pass, the business of the border crossings from Alaska continued without reprieve. The new arrivals, having survived their ascent of the Dead Horse Trail, had their supplies checked, customs duties collected, and the health of their pack horses assessed before being allowed to continue their journey into the Dominion of Canada. Day in and day out, the work continued and was managed with military precision and emotional detachment.

The door to the cabin opened with a squeak, and Constable Stephen Grant stepped inside, closing the door behind him to keep the chill at bay. He was dressed in the full uniform of the North-West Mounted Police, red serge jacket, dark trousers with a broad yellow stripe running down each leg, the wide-brimmed Biltmore Stetson, and knee-high black leather riding boots that had been well-worn from his travels. His face was clean shaven and the scar that ran across his left cheekbone to his jawline was still healing. It had faded from its once angry red to a deeper pink. It was the kind of scar that men spoke about in hushed tones, an indicator of a man who had survived a dangerous encounter and lived through something most others couldn't even fathom. His quiet confidence, coupled with the scar, gave Grant a cold and dangerous aura that made others wary at first glance. His deep-set green eyes revealed a sharp awareness of the changing circumstances around him that came with every new order.

Formerly of the Tagish Post, he had saved every man in the Pass during the recent attack by the outlaw gang and had become a well-liked figure of the detachment since Strickland seconded him to remain there under his command.

"Good morning, Inspector," Grant said as he stomped the snow from his boots.

"Morning Grant," Strickland responded, glancing up briefly from the pile of papers in front of him. He gestured for Grant to sit.

Grant took a seat across from Strickland, his posture rigid and attentive. He had known Strickland for only a short time now and the older man was a career officer: efficient, no-nonsense, and always focused on the task at hand. However, today there was something about the current situation that seemed to add a layer of tension to his demeanour.

"I'm all but ready to head for Skagway," Grant said, getting straight to the point. "I've thought about who to take with me-"

"Let me stop you there," Strickland said. He leant forward, folding his hands in front of him. His expression remained calm, but there was an air of finality in his voice when he spoke.

"Superintendent Steele has re-evaluated the situation and taken matters into his own hands. You and Thompson will be heading down to Bennett Lake instead."

Grant raised an eyebrow, his curiosity piqued. "Bennett?"

"That's right. You'll be taking the duties there, at which point you'll be attached to a greater operation." Strickland's gaze hardened as he continued, "Inspector Zachary Wood will transport all the collected territorial duties to Victoria, via Skagway. Steele has requested your presence to join the mission and help Wood navigate the, ahem, landscape."

Grant processed the information for a moment, as he considered the new task ahead. He'd heard the name Zachary Wood before but had never met the man. "Who exactly is this Wood?"

Strickland's gaze softened for a moment, almost as if he were measuring his words carefully. "He's a seasoned officer, Constable. He's sharp, disciplined, and most importantly he knows how to handle himself in tough situations. I expect you to support him fully on this. The operation is critical. As you know, the route is far from safe. That's why Steele wants you involved. I have little doubt that your experience with Soapy Smith's gang and their tactics will come in handy."

Grant nodded, his mind already beginning to picture the logistical details. Skagway was a dangerous place, dominated by criminals and lawlessness. Soapy Smith's gang would be a constant threat. The original mission held a lot of moving parts, and now to transport even more money out? It would take someone with both intelligence and strength of character to keep it all together. He hoped Wood was just such a man.

"What's changed?" Grant asked. "Why are we diverting to Bennett instead of continuing from here and on through to Skagway instead?"

Strickland's expression grew serious. "Steele believes that if we stick to the original plan, we'll be walking right into their hands. Smith is no fool; he'll know exactly what we're carrying and where we're headed. By taking the Chilkoot instead? It may give us a better chance of staying out of his direct line of sight."

Grant paused. He thought a man like Soapy Smith would stop at nothing to take what wasn't his. This would be a delicate operation. He couldn't afford to be careless, not with so much at stake. "That makes sense," he replied.

The cabin door creaked open behind Grant, and he felt winter's cold kiss across the nape of his neck. He shivered involuntarily from its insistent peck.

Strickland reached into a drawer, removed an envelope and slid it across the desk toward Grant.

"Your orders," he said. "Once you arrive in Bennett, you and Thompson will meet Wood and assist him however he needs. After you get him safely to Skagway and he boards his ship out with all the money, then you are back on mission." Strickland nodded in his head towards Grant's shoulder as he continued, "You'll liaise with Staff Sergeant Hyles here and then assess how best to handle the accumulated post and mail down there." He then introduced the two men, and said, "Staff Sergeant, this is Constable Grant."

Grant stood up from his chair and turned to meet Sergeant Hyles. He was a solid, imposing figure, with the kind of quiet presence that draws attention without effort. Standing well over six feet tall, his broad shoulders and muscular build gave him an air of authority, his very posture commanding immediate respect.

His face, though not as weathered as some of the older men in the force, bore the hard edge of someone who's seen enough to know that this world isn't kind. His skin was fair but marred by deep lines around his eyes and mouth, evidence of the stress and hardships he had endured in his years with the Mounted Police. His brown eyes were steady and watchful, nothing escaped his notice. They carried a weight of experience, sharp and calculating, as though he was always thinking two steps ahead.

"James Hyles, good to meet you," the older man said and offered Grant his hand.

"Stephen Grant, you as well," he replied, shaking the Sergeant's hand. "How do you find Skagway?"

"Skag is disagreeable," Hyles replied. "Most disagreeable. It's likely the roughest place on Earth."

"How much mail are we talking about?"

"Piles, heaps, not far off a small hillock's worth," Hyles said. "Aye, it grows with ever new steamer that pulls into the harbour. This mail? It's more dangerous than any bag of coins."

"I don't follow," Grant remarked.

"Information is currency. It's power. When you're so far from anything resembling proper civilization, the smallest slip of paper can have consequences," Hyles replied, his voice gaining conviction as he continued. "That letter from a mining prospector might contain the key to a claim, even the deed itself. A note from some settler in Dawson might be telling someone when the next riverboat is due, whether our outposts have received reinforcements, whether a gold heist has come off, or not. Or that someone's parent has died, and an inheritance awaits. Maybe it's a message home or a message from our government telling us to fight the Americans. You get the picture?"

"I hear what you're saying." Grant's mind was working as he considered the Staff Sergeant's words. "I hadn't considered that. I'll be happy to help."

"Grand, because the thing is, Soapy Smith's goons have been eyeing the docks for months now. They'd love to get their hands on it."

"There's plenty to coordinate," Grant replied as his fingers traced the edges of the letter holding his orders. "The quicker we get it moving, the better." Absorbing these new details, he knew he was ready for this task. The uncertainty, the danger, it was all part of the job. It always had been.

"One more thing, Grant," Strickland added, his voice dropping slightly in tone. "I want you to keep an eye on Wood. He is a capable officer, but he will need you to back him up. Trust is essential in these kinds of operations, especially when things go sideways."

Grant met Strickland's eyes and heard the unspoken message. He knew what it meant. The success of this mission depended on their ability to work together, to anticipate each other's movements, and to cover each other when the time came. In the unforgiving expanse of the wilderness, there was little room for hesitation or doubt.

"I'll keep that in mind, sir," Grant said firmly.

Strickland stood up from his desk, extending his hand. "Good. You leave within the hour."

Grant shook Strickland's offered hand, giving a firm nod before exiting the cabin.

As he walked past the outpost's Maxim machine gun nest, his boots crunched over the snow-laden ground. He had seen the bulky machine in action before and it was a death dealing beast that lay in wait for the opportunity to roar once again. He hoped he would never have to hear it barking in anger ever again. The gun felt out of place, just like the idea that he and the men around him were somehow meant to bring order to a world that wanted none. Still, it was just a tool. A necessary one. Just like the rest of them: tools, cogs in the wheels of justice and order.

Grant headed toward the stables where he knew Thompson would be. The young Constable had already been preparing to accompany him down to Skagway, but now that the mission had shifted, it was time to change course.

They would still be traversing dangerous territory, but this was the life of a Mountie: a life defined by constant change, rapid decision-making and an unyielding sense of duty.

Inside, Thompson was working on one of the horses, brushing its coat with methodical strokes. He looked up as Grant entered and wiped his hands on a cloth.

"Thompson," Grant greeted the young Constable. "Change of plans. Get your things. We're heading to Bennett."

Thompson's eyes widened slightly in surprise. "Bennett? I thought we were going to Skagway."

"We were. We are, but the mission's shifted." Grant paused and watched Thompson carefully. "Get packed. We're leaving right away."

Thompson didn't hesitate, "I'll be ready."

Grant turned on his heel and made his way to the barracks to collect his effects. His mind was already shifting to the next phase of the operation. In the Klondike, nothing ever went according to plan. The Mounties had learned that long ago. All they could do was move forward: swiftly, cautiously, and with an unwavering resolve.

CHAPTER III

The Path Ahead

Bennett greeted Grant and Thompson with the typical harshness of a northern spring's morning. A chill lingered in the fog bound air as they approached the lakeside town. Their Buffalo Coats were rolled and stowed with on their saddle packs and the thaw had made the trails out of the foothills slick and slippery. Rivulets of brown muck made for a tricky descent, forcing the horses to slog their way through it, their hooves sinking into the deep, soggy ground. As a result, the two Mounties and their mounts arrived at their destination splattered and caked in mud and slush. Grant's red serge, usually immaculate, or at least close to it, was stained dark with wet dirt, and the sharp lines of his uniform were lost under the weight of the grime that clung to him.

Thompson's mood, as ever, was more buoyant than Grant's. He didn't mind the mess at all. He grinned beneath the caked dirt on his face and was already looking forward to the stables, where the scent of straw and hay would bring some relief after the damp, unpleasant journey.

He had not travelled down from White Pass before and the young Mountie found Bennett a busy, bustling place. This semblance of a town lived off chaos as gold seekers, Stampeders, and boatbuilders packed themselves close to the shores of the lake. It felt like a place on the edge of something big, where the energy simmered just below the surface.

"Quite the scene, isn't it?" Thompson remarked, his voice brighter than the morning sun.

"Anything's an improvement from the Log Cabin," Grant replied with a grunt.

While they rode on, passing row after row of tents where men were huddled together, cooking, packing supplies or working with a fervour to finish their boats. Some had fashioned rough wooden shanties out of hand-milled lumber not used on the boats. The smell of wood and tar filled the air. Every available space in Bennett seemed to be taken up by those who had arrived to quest for their fortune. Some were hammering together questionable looking hulls, while others struggled to drag their readied craft down to the makeshift docks on the frigid waters of the lake that was still loosening itself from the ice. The chatter, the hammering, the shouts across the shores, all blended into a cacophony of noise as the Mounties made their way through the cluttered encampment. Bennett felt alive, like a boiling pot ready to spill over, when in fact it was merely a waypoint, a place where people had come to rest, refuel, and make last-minute plans before pushing on toward the promised riches further north.

When the NWMP Outpost came in sight, Grant remarked how the barracks itself were nothing special: a large, utilitarian structure behind a rough palisade that would not resist much of an assault. It was built merely to shelter the small force of Constables stationed here from the constant elements. The stables were just as rudimentary, its rough-hewn logs formed more of a wind break for the animals than a proper structure, but it served its purpose as well as could be expected.

Thompson lifted a hand to his eyes as he squinted through the morning fog. “Stables! Oh joy,” he chuckled to himself.

"Take care of the horses,” Grant directed Thompson as he reined his mount in beside the stables. “They’re looking half-drowned in this muck. I’ll go and find Inspector Wood.”

Thompson nodded and dismounted with his usual verve, heading straight for the stables without another word.

Grant watched Thompson go, shaking his head with a slight grin of his own. He didn’t mind the rough terrain, the muck or sleeping rough. He had never been one to shy away from hard work, he just didn’t do it with Thompson’s effortless smile.

As he moved toward the barracks, he passed several Constables grouped around a large campfire. A battered blackened pot was suspended over the fire, hanging from a wrought iron tripod. The gathered Constables were passing around steaming mugs.

"Where do I find Inspector Wood?" Grant asked the group.

One of the Constables, a young man with a rough face replied, "Wood? I think he's in the office, rear of the barracks."

Grant grunted and gave a curt nod in thanks.

The wooden door creaked as he entered the barracks and the familiar scent of burning wood and packed earth took over his senses. The main room was cramped, with neat rows of cots running its length. The rough-hewn wood walls were lined with shelves containing equipment, spare uniforms, weapons racks and other supplies. The temperature was warmer than the outside, but just barely. A few Mounties were huddled by a central woodstove, warming their hands. A few heads turned, but seeing the red serge uniform of the new arrival, most simply nodded before they returned to their low, murmured conversations.

Grant didn't stop to greet them. Instead, he moved quickly past, his eyes scanning the interior until he saw the doorway at the rear of the room.

When he reached the small office Grant saw two men inside, standing by a desk with their backs to the door. They were studying a map of the Klondike. One was tracing a route across the Chilkoot Trail route towards the Alaskan coast. Grant could see that both men's uniforms were perfectly maintained, every crease sharp, every button polished. There was no sign of the mud or chaos that seemed to follow Grant wherever he went. He then saw the intricate gold braiding on the uniform of the larger man's shoulders and sleeves that denoted a Superintendent. He had never met Sam Steele, but the man's legend was well known to every Mountie.

"Constable Grant, reporting," he announced himself.

"Grant," Steele said as he turned, his voice deep and commanding, his stance rigid and military. "Good to see you."

Grant's gaze flickered over to Wood, standing beside the map.

"Inspector Wood, I presume?" Grant asked.

Wood didn't immediately acknowledge Grant, his eyes remained fixed on the map. When he did turn to look at Grant, he offered a thin smile, but there was little warmth in it.

"Constable," he said, in a clipped, businesslike tone. He was already evaluating the new arrival. "Is it your usual practice to report in such a condition?"

Grant looked down at his filthy jacket and the mud splattered across the rest of his uniform, and offered, "Spring thaw made for a mucky descent. Given the urgent business at hand, I thought it better to present myself and then clean up afterward. Constable Thompson's taking care of the horses," Grant added. "We'll be ready to move out as soon as you give the order."

Wood turned away and as he did, the corner of his mouth pulled into a sneer. He returned his gaze to the map without further comment. There was an edge to Wood, a sharpness in the way he carried himself. Grant could feel tension appear between them, something unspoken, and it hung heavy in the air.

Steele, took charge, and said, "Too right Grant. We'll keep this brief," he said, motioning for them all to sit. "We're facing a delicate situation, and I'll need your best work. As you're aware, Constable, we're moving a large sum of money. It's critical that we maintain security and secrecy along the route, especially when it comes to Skagway."

Wood did not sit right away, but when he did his posture was straight and his demeanour remained as cold as the outdoors. There was something about the man, something Grant couldn't quite put his finger on. Maybe it was the way Wood seemed to evaluate every move and read every unspoken word. He'd served with all manner of officers and was familiar with the type who focused more on presentation, grooming and drill than practical matters, like staying alive. He was beginning to suspect Wood might be one of those types.

When Wood spoke, his even voice was calculating, "Skagway will be a problem. Smith has eyes everywhere. We can't afford to take our time or draw any undue attention to ourselves."

Grant nodded, already anticipating the challenges ahead. "If keep our heads down," he replied. "If we plan the route carefully and avoid any hotspots, places where Smith's men are likely to be it would be best. I presume that's why you're considering using the Chilkoot Trail?"

"Your presumption would be correct," Steele said, his voice carrying a firmness that cut through the tension. "We need to be three steps ahead of Smith and make sure our approach doesn't give him anything to work with. He's not just some thug, he's clever."

"Can we travel out of uniform to blend in?"

"Certainly not!" came Wood's snappish reply.

"I'd prefer we remained official and uniformed," Steele added.

Grant shifted in his chair, his hand resting casually on the top of his holster. "In that case," he offered, after a long pause. "I have an idea that might help,"

Both Steele and Wood looked at him, the latter's expression becoming slightly pinched.

"What if we can mislead Smith's gang?" Grant suggested, his gaze steady. "It's clear that he's watching everything we do. But, if we can make him believe that Inspector Wood has been recalled to headquarters, perhaps even make it appear like any shipment has been delayed? It might buy enough time to slip past." He let that suggestion hang in the air for a moment.

Wood raised an eyebrow, the scepticism in his expression was clear. "How exactly would you propose we mislead him?" he asked, his voice cool.

Grant met his gaze. "There are plenty of ways. Word can get out, little pieces of information, whispers and rumours placed in the right ears. It's not as hard as you might think. People talk, especially when they think something big is happening. Staff Sergeant Hyles is in White Pass and hasn't returned to Skagway yet. We could get him to talk loosely when he returns there. No doubt it'll reach Soapy's ears."

Steele nodded thoughtfully, clearly considering the plan. "It's a possibility. It's a risk. If Smith catches wind that this is a deception, he'll know the shipment is on the move and then tighten his grip everywhere."

Grant didn't flinch, "Every plan is risky, sir. If we can make him think we've lost our edge or are overconfident, he'll believe that."

Wood was nonchalant and observed, "He's slippery but I don't think we're dealing with some criminal mastermind here. Aren't we giving him a little too much credit?"

Grant didn't care for the challenge in Wood's words, the subtle insinuation that he didn't understand their opponent. His experience with Smith's tactics gave him an edge. But instead of responding immediately, he allowed his gaze to shift to Steele, hoping for some support from command.

"I wouldn't underestimate him," Grant countered. "We can't be certain of what Smith might be planning. Or presume what he might believe. However, I believe we can count on him having ears everywhere. Disinformation could be an advantage."

There was a brief pause before Steele spoke again. "I think Grant's idea has merit," he said. "If we can mislead Smith's men, give them something to chase, we can move the money before they have a chance to react."

Wood exhaled slowly, clearly not convinced. "I don't like deception," he muttered, more to himself than anyone else. "It leaves too much room for error."

Grant's patience was wearing thin, but he kept his voice even. "Sometimes, you have to play their game. No one expects us, the Mounties, to lie. It's not the perfect cover, but it might work."

"I still don't like it," Wood said, his eyes hardening.

"Wood," Steele interjected sharply. "We don't have the luxury of liking everything that comes our way. We have a job to do. The money must make it to Victoria, intact. End of story."

There was a long silence. Wood looked like he was about to argue again, but instead, he simply nodded curtly. "Understood, sir," he said, his tone stiff.

Steele smiled, as if pleased with the appearance of resolution. "Good. Then let's get to work. Grant, you're in charge of spreading the rumours around. Wood, you'll continue with the other details."

Grant nodded, his mind already moving on to the next stage of the plan. The tension between him and Wood was palpable, but he couldn't afford to let it distract him. This wasn't about personal grudges it was about mission success. As far as Grant was concerned, that meant making it past Smith's gang at all costs. Wood's opinion or ego be damned.

As the meeting wound down, Grant rose from his chair, his still healing leg muscles stiff from sitting too long.

"We'll need a solid backup plan," Wood said, glancing at Steele. "Just in case."

Steele's gaze never wavered. "You'll have it. Dismissed."

Wood didn't say anything further, he just watched as Grant made his way toward the door. There was no warmth in the man's eyes, no sign of trust.

When Grant stepped out into the cold air, he knew that when it came down to it, he was more than willing to do whatever was required to get the job done. Whether Wood was on his side or not, there would be no turning back. A new and deadly game of cat and mouse between the Mounties and Soapy Smith had begun in earnest.

CHAPTER IV

The Reunion

As Grant walked the muddy paths that wound through the tent encampment forming the 'town' of Bennett, he could smell the wood smoke, the pungent scent of wet earth, and the sharp tang of the lake whose icy waters lead towards the broader Yukon itself. The camp hummed with an unrestrained and frenetic energy, a mixture of hope and anxiety. The Stampeders were nervous but determined and as their anxieties grew, so did the sound of hammering, shouting, and the creaking of timbers being forced into place, one after another.

Heavy clumps of the thawing ground stuck to the soles of Grant's boots, but he hardly noticed as he stomped and slid his way through the heart of the town. While the people around him were absorbed by the chase for gold; he was just as absorbed by the mission to get this shipment of money safely out of the territory.

Preoccupied with his thoughts, he continued to ruminate over how something just felt 'off'. As he considered the dangerous trek over the mountains to Skagway, traversing into and through Soapy Smith's territory, the potential unknowns worried him as much as the phantom criminals that could be lurking around every corner. In his mind, these faceless villains waited in the shadows to strike at them and steal their precious cargo.

He wondered, had McCade feel this way when his gang were transporting their stolen gold from the Dawson heist? The Constable reflected on the mindset of his recent foe, the man who had left him scarred but ended up separated from his gold, and dead to boot, all thanks to his unquenchable thirst for revenge against Grant.

He was so caught up in his thoughts that he almost didn't recognize the horse and rider approaching him. The rider was an unimposing figure wrapped in a long, weather-beaten poncho. A broad-brimmed hat shaded his face, but there was something familiar about the shape of the man's shoulders, the way he sat in saddle with a quiet confidence. And then, as they drew closer, Grant left his thoughts behind as he placed him.

"Jorge?" Grant called out, his voice rising above the clamour of the camp.

The man paused as his dark eyes looked towards Grant. A grin of recognition spread across his face, the kind of smile that meant a genuine greeting from someone who didn't often see familiar faces. Jorge's slight frame was unmistakable even under the layers of shabby clothing, his long poncho was patched in places, his boots worn but sturdy. His black hair, usually a bit wild, was tied back tightly behind his head. There was no mistaking the Mexican long rider, he was one of the few people beyond his fellow Mounties that Grant trusted without question. The first time they had crossed paths, Jorge helped Grant by carrying a message to the detachment in this town. They had since struck up a loose friendship of sorts, one built on shared dangers and a mutual respect.

"Ola Constable," Jorge said, his voice thick with the drawl of someone accustomed to long days alone in the saddle. "I did not expect to see you here, my friend."

Grant couldn't help but smile, relieved to see a face he knew in this sea of strangers around him. He reached up to shake Jorge's hand. "I thought you'd be far away by now, up to Dawson and presiding over your own northern El Dorado. It's good to see you."

Jorge laughed and pushing his hat back, ran a hand through his hair. His dark eyes scanned the busy scene around them. "Ah, well, you know how it is, amigo. The open trail calls to me, and sometimes it brings you right back to where you started." Jorge nodded towards the bustling camp around them, as people hammered and shouted at each other in the mad rush towards the final stretch of their journeys to Dawson City, "What brings you through this mess?"

"I'm glad to say I'm not here to inspect the seaworthiness of these boats," Grant replied.

"I would hope not," Jorge shot back. "You'd never leave this place. I've seen better boats sink in a puddle."

Grant laughed, feeling a small knot of tension loosen in his chest. "I'm starting to think the same thing. You seem to turn up at all the right moments for me. You've been working the trails?"

"Si, hauling mostly," Jorge replied, "Food, Medicines, supplies. Everyone is in a hurry to get to Dawson, but nobody wants to spend time going back and forth. Not me."

"I could use a man like you right now, to be honest."

Jorge's smile faded slightly as his sharp eyes scanned the Mountie. "What's the matter, amigo? You look like you're dealing with more than the usual mess of these Stampeders."

Grant nodded, glancing around them. "I have to move a shipment across the Chilkoot and meet a ship going to Victoria."

"That's not so hard," Jorge quipped.

"It gets more complicated when certain people in Skagway hear it will be moving through their territory."

Jorge raised an eyebrow, his eyes flickering with interest. "Amigo-amigo-amigo, Skagway? That is a hard town, full of danger. You need more than just guns to get through there."

Grant met his eyes, his expression serious. "I know. That's why I need you."

"Would this be about that thief, Soapy Smith?"

"We're trying to keep this quiet, but Soapy's going to find out about it sooner or later." Grant replied, his voice dropping into hushed tones. "I need to get to Skagway without drawing too much attention."

Jorge didn't answer immediately. He looked around the camp, his sharp eyes taking in the movement of men, the horses, the hustle and bustle. His mind was clearly working and Grant thought perhaps he was weighing over his options for escape. The long rider was a man who preferred working alone and travelling on his own terms.

After another moment, Jorge asked, "What do you need?"

Grant didn't shy away from the question. "I need to spread a rumour."

Clearly intrigued but not fully convinced, Jorge asked, "What kind of rumour?"

"The Inspector in command is a man named Wood. I want it to get around that Wood's being recalled to Ottawa. He'll be travelling under escort then taking passage on a ship."

"Why would this man be taken out under escort?"

"It would have to be something bad, theft?" Grant answered, and added, "Taking bribes would be better, I think Soapy would understand that. He'd even like it."

Jorge studied him for a moment, rubbing his chin thoughtfully. "Si, that would make sense. They say this Soapy is a tricky one. It must be believable, or he won't be fooled."

"I know. That's why I need you to carry this message for me," Grant said and paused before continuing. "I need you to spread the message around here before you go to White Pass. Tell Strickland I sent you to connect with Sergeant Hyles. He'll be heading down to Skagway. Can you go with him and spread the rumour there as well?

"You want me to go to Skagway as well? Over the Dead Horse Trail, again?"

"Yes, please Jorge. I don't trust anyone else."

Jorge was silent for a moment, his gaze distant. He was clearly considering the risk. "That's a tricky number. I have costs. This isn't like the last time I carried your message."

"When I get to Skagway, I'll make it up to you. I have another mission there and I'll need help with transporting a big shipment of mail back here. I can pay you then."

There was a long pause as Jorge considered it, "Once you reach Skagway, how do you plan to get past the gang?"

"That'll be my problem, you don't need to worry about that."

"I want to get paid. So, I worry. You think this rumour will keep them off the trail long enough for you to slip through?"

Grant nodded. "That's the idea."

Jorge stared at him for a while longer, and just as Grant began to think he might turn him down, Jorge finally let out a long sigh and shook his head, a small, amused smile tugging at his lips.

"All right," he said. "If it helps keep you and your cargo safe, I'll do it. I'll head to White Pass, find this Sergeant Hyles, and carry your message to Skagway."

Grant let out a breath he hadn't realized he'd been holding, "Thank you, Jorge. You've just made this a lot easier."

Jorge tipped his hat, giving him a short nod. "Don't thank me just yet. We haven't haggled over my fee yet. The hard part's just beginning. You keep your head down and make sure this Wood stays on course. I will see you in Skagway."

"I will see you there," Grant said, feeling a relief wash over him. "Stay safe, my friend."

Grant knew the risks well enough. Soapy Smith's network was vast, and any little slip-up could cost them everything. With the charismatic Jorge churning the rumour mill as he travelled to the coast, he was confident that the story would spread and get to Skagway. If the right people heard his lies, they might have a fighting chance.

As Grant walked back towards the detachment, he couldn't help but feel that despite this progress, the journey ahead was about to become even more complicated than he'd initially thought.

CHAPTER V

A Rough Start

"You did *what*?" Wood's voice boomed out across the outpost's main yard, each word a thunderclap of fury. His fists were clenched at his sides, his face flushed, eyes blazing with anger.

Standing in the middle of the detachment's busy yard, Grant straightened, keeping his own composure as he met Wood's furious gaze. He knew this confrontation was coming, but that didn't make it any easier. He had barely set foot in the outpost when Wood confronted him for an update on how he planned to spread the rumours he had been tasked with.

"You heard me," Grant replied with a hint of steel in his words. "It's all a ruse to throw off Smith's people. Obviously, none of it is true."

Wood took a step toward him, his boots digging into the wet earth with an angry squelch. "It's not your name being dragged through this mud! Recalled? For bribery? I have worked my entire life to earn my reputation, and you've sullied it with one little walk around town. You think Soapy Smith, of all people, will fall for some fabricated tale about me?"

Grant's jaw tightened. "The man thrives on corruption. He sees the bad in people, it's entirely plausible. Removing the man from his post? Under an armed guard? 'You know those Mounties, those do-gooder Canadians', they'll say. A little disinformation, a little confusion? He'll bite. That's all we need to buy a short window to get in and get you on that ship."

Wood's face twisted with a mixture of disbelief and contempt. He crossed his arms tightly over his chest. "You're gambling with my life, Grant. With all our lives, frankly. There's no way he'll believe I have gone down for taking bribes. That's the most reckless thing I've heard in a long time."

Grant's fists clenched at his sides as Wood's words stung. He wasn't exactly wrong, but Grant wasn't about to back down.

"Does Soapy Smith know you personally?" Grant said through gritted teeth. When he did not receive an immediate reply, he continued, "No, exactly. He presumes to know who we are and what we're all like. He thinks we're sticks in the mud and those sticks go halfway up our own asses. To him we're superior, arrogant and elitist policemen. In his mind, we would certainly overreact to something as simple, to him, as bribery and graft. I'm not just playing some guessing game here, Inspector." Grant was in full flow as he spoke, hammering his points home. "I'm trying, we, are trying to keep that cargo out of Soapy's hands. If we don't do something to misdirect him, we're just sitting ducks."

Wood took another step forward, his face inches from Grant's, "You don't get to decide how this operation goes. And, sure as hell, you don't get to make me look like some criminal in front of everyone else." He paused, his eyes narrowing. "I'm in charge. Not you."

The heat in his chest flared, but Grant refused to give in to it. He had been through worse. He had fought for survival on this godforsaken frontier, and if Wood thought he could intimidate him with a few hard words, he had another thing coming.

"You're right. I'm not in charge, sir," Grant replied, his voice tinged with something that wasn't quite disrespect but was at least measured.

"Don't ever try to pull something like that again," Wood said, spitting the words out with venom.

Grant's voice was steady but full of that edge, the one that warned people to back off. "I did what had to be done. The truth doesn't always work in our favour. Sometimes you have to make it your own."

Wood's eyes flashed as he turned his head, locking eyes with Grant, and for a moment, it seemed like the world had gone still around them. As both men glared at each other, the distance between them became both literal and figurative.

"Right now, that's exactly what we need, sir."

"If we're going to get this done, we'll need to work together," Wood said, his voice quiet but still laced with tension. "You can't just make decisions on your own without considering the risks."

Grant was about to respond, but at that moment, Superintendent Steele approached, his heavy boots sliding through the mud. His presence was a welcome interruption for Grant. Wood's gaze flicked to Steele for a moment, but there was no hiding the tension in his posture.

Steele stepped forward, his hands clasped behind his back as he took in the scene. "I trust I'm not interrupting anything too important?"

Both men, still simmering with their respective frustrations, turned to face their superior officer. Wood straightened, clearly trying to regain some semblance of control. "No, sir. Just discussing the logistics of the mission."

Grant nodded sharply, though his eyes were still fixed on Wood, "That's one way to put it."

Steele raised an eyebrow but chose not to delve into the growing tension. Instead, he glanced around at the camp, taking note of the other Constables who had returned their attention from the scene to their various duties. He gestured toward the other men in Wood's party: Constables Chalmers, Young, and Thompson. Each was busy with their own tasks, preparing for the journey ahead. He inquired, "The men look ready to move. Everything set for departure?"

Grant shifted his attention to Steele, grateful for the break from the confrontation with Wood. "We should be moving out in the morning. The earlier we can get across the Chilkoot and onto the coast, the better."

Steele nodded but then looked back to Wood, who had fallen silent. "You'll need to move carefully," the Superintendent said. "How's our disinformation campaign shaping up?"

Grant replied, "It's already underway. Right, Inspector?"

Wood nodded curtly, his face still tight with frustration.

"We're ready when you are," Grant said, before saluting Steele. "If there's nothing else, Superintendent? I'll be in the stables."

"Very well," Stele replied and returned the salute.

Grant turned toward the stables. He couldn't help but feel a sense of resentment. It was clear that Wood wasn't ready to let go of his anger or his doubts about Grant's methods and capabilities. As much as he disliked Wood's attitude, as much as the man's arrogance grated on him, they were in this together.

At the stables, Thompson had already finished preparing the animals and had been double-checking their gear, looking anxious to be on their way. The dunnage bags filled with the precious gold and money were being securely packed and would be spread across each of the five Mountie's horses.

As Grant took a deep breath to bleed off the emotions from his clash with Wood a new voice called out, "You're always in the middle of a problem, aren't you Constable?"

Grant exhaled before he composed himself for a fresh confrontation. He turned to see Sergent Flynn, Bennett's Quartermaster standing at the stable's entrance.

"Sergeant, always a pleasure to see you."

"What have you got yourself involved with this time?"

"There's a question for the ages. I'm not entirely sure myself."

"You're going with Wood? Why Steele trusts you is beyond me," the Sergeant quipped.

"I don't think he trusts me. I'm just doing my job and going where I'm ordered to go."

"Well, I don't bloody trust you. Period."

"Full stop. You've made that abundantly clear and thank you for sharing your views, Sergeant. Now, if you don't mind? I've got some preparations to handle," Grant said, "No doubt you do as well."

He held Flynn's stare. Not detecting any further incoming rebuke, only then did he turn his back on the Sergeant. He had practised this as an effective method to not be flagrant in his disobedience with superiors he did not agree with who had not yet dismissed him.

"One day Grant, good will out." Flynn offered before he left the stables.

Thompson watched the Sergeant leave before he leant towards Grant and asked, "What was that about?"

"A long story that's short on meaning. Don't worry yourself about it." He replied and returned to looking over his tack. The tone communicated enough to the younger Constable not to ask any follow up questions on the subject.

The following morning, with everything packed and the horses saddled, the group gathered near the edge of the camp, ready to depart. The weather was cool, with heavy clouds hanging low in the sky, but at least it hadn't started raining yet.

Wood rode up on his horse, his posture still rigid, his face a mask of resolve. He didn't meet Grant's eyes as he approached, though Grant could feel the heat of his glare from a distance.

"Ready?" Wood asked curtly.

Grant met his gaze, locking eyes for a moment. "As ready as we're going to be," he replied.

And with that, they set off. The journey towards the Chilkoot Trail began in silence. The group rode steadily, their horses picking their way through the mud and the remaining snow that still clung to the trail. Grant was focused on the path ahead, his thoughts constantly returning to the task at hand: getting the cargo to Skagway without drawing the attention of Soapy Smith's gang.

But with the weight of their cargo, the sourness of the argument, and the dangers of the trail looming ahead, Grant couldn't shake the feeling that things were about to get much worse before they got better.

CHAPTER VI

The Chilkoot

The rain fell in relentless torrents. Those grey curtains obscured the peaks of the towering mountains to the west. The trail up the slopes of the Chilkoot was difficult, but not yet treacherous. The muddy, waterlogged surface of the trails was broken by series upon series of ruts and slick rocks. The air was thick with mist, and dampness had crept into the clothes, bones, and the very thoughts of the Mounties. The team had been climbing without pause, the weight of the dunnage bags pressing down on their horses. The continuous uphill stretch combined with the weather was a becoming a physical and mental grind. The Chilkoot Trail held an infamous reputation, and their passage had not yet reached its difficult stages.

However, Grant's mind was elsewhere. His thoughts kept returning to the tension between him and Inspector Wood. The conversation with Superintendent Steele had gone over well enough, but as the days had passed since leaving Bennett, the friction and subtle animosity between him and Wood had only grown.

The rumour that Grant had spread, though carefully devised and deliberately subtle, had brewed problems. Wood had taken it poorly when he'd first heard. Bribery charges? That was a dangerous accusation to throw around, especially for a man like Wood who was intent on protecting his reputation. Despite the Inspector's protests, Grant did understand the risks involved. It had been necessary to set the lie, to make it seem like Wood was in trouble and was being recalled to Ottawa due to misconduct. It wasn't about undermining Wood's authority on the mission, it was about keeping the gold out of Soapy Smith's hands.

Thompson rode ahead of the group, his mount picking its way carefully through the muck. Grant kept his pace steady, not allowing his eyes to wander. His mind kept returning to the trail ahead, and to Soapy Smith. Would the gang be waiting for them somewhere ahead? Or would the rumour Grant had spread about Wood give them the breathing room they desperately needed?

The trails were difficult, the horses were struggling, their hooves slipping in the muck, their breathing laboured as they climbed higher along the trail. There was little conversation as the group pressed onwards.

Grant caught sight of Wood ahead of him in the queue of their loose formation. He was riding steadily, his posture rigid, a man weighed down by his own sense of duty. However, Grant knew that beneath the surface, there was something more at play between them. Wood was not a fan of Grant's methods. The suspicion was mutual, though neither of them had outright voiced it yet. For all his experience and authority, Wood still had doubts about Grant's ability to handle the situation. Grant wasn't certain whether Wood was truly the right type of man to lead this mission.

As they continued upwards, the trail twisted and turned, the rocky terrain forcing them to slow their pace. Wood decided to keep their profile as low as possible, they would avoid the sprawling tent encampment of Lindeman City. It lay at the southernmost edge of a Lake of the same name, it was connected to Bennett Lake by a short river. Much like Bennett, the inhabitants were in full boat building mode. Virtually every tree in its vicinity had been cut down and its scar was expanding outwards as more wood was hauled to town to meet the demand for boat materials and firewood.

The plan was for the team to make their way across the Chilkoot Trail and then down to Dyea in Alaska. From there, the final leg of their journey was to ferry their payload across the short stretch of water to Skagway, and their destination: a berthed ship that would travel Wood and the money down the coast to Victoria. Grant knew better than to let his focus slip. No matter how far they travelled, no matter how many twists and turns lay ahead, they were never going to be out of danger. Not while Soapy Smith and his gang were still in the picture.

Despite giving Lindeman City a wide berth, there was no way to avoid the steady flow of traffic coming eastbound and down from the Chilkoot. The sheer weight and volume of the gear being hauled past them was evident in the slow, laborious pace the descending Stampeders maintained. Most were dragging wooden toboggan-style sleds behind them, groaning as they struggled over the uneven ground. These sleds were weighed down with the critical supplies they'll need for survival in the Klondike. They carried canned food, dry rations, flour, rice, bacon, and sacks of beans. Those staples would have to last for months as they journeyed through the wilderness. The heavier items, like cast-iron stoves, cooking pots, or axes, were strapped down or lashed to the sides of their sleds, making the hauling even more difficult. In the relentless spring rains, the weight of their equipment seemed to grow heavier by the minute despite rain-slicked slopes lubricating their progress.

Young and old, from all walks of life, men and women alike were hunched under the weight of their "ton of goods", the requisite load of one thousand pounds each of them must carry to meet the Canadian government's demands. This was no light task. Some had packed their gear with precision, with the weight distributed across multiple bags, boxes, and crates. Others had not. Despite the precision and preparation, everyone struggled.

As Grant watched those passing by, he considered their faces. He saw a mixture of gruff resolve and silent fatigue. Some were hardened by the weeks of toil, their eyes determined beneath heavy brows, while others were younger, more hopeful, their steps buoyed by excitement and the dream of striking it rich. The rain poured down unrelenting, collecting in the crevices of their coats, making their packs even heavier. Mud clung to their boots, their clothes were stained and dripping, but they marched on, driven by the promise of gold.

Out of all the traffic crossing the border that Grant had witnessed, he had not truly considered what happened after they left the snow bound places. Sleds and horses had been the norm crossing at White Pass, but here on the Chilkoot, other than local horse traffic from the eastern side of the mountains, they had not seen any Stampeders with horse powered assistance. It was just the sleds and bulky leather packs tied to their own backs, bulging with tools essential for the harsh conditions ahead: shovels, pickaxes, frying pans, lanterns, and rope. Tents, compressed into small, cumbersome rolls, dangling from the sides of their sleds or hanging from their backs. This was not just a journey to find gold; it was an attempt to survive the unforgiving wilderness with nothing more than what they could carry, what they could haul.

Grant glanced away from the passing tide of humanity and looked towards the brooding figure of Wood, riding ahead with quiet determination. If anything, they would need to rely on each other more than ever. For the sake of the cargo. For the sake of keeping the peace in the North. But even Grant knew that peace in the Klondike was fragile and fleeting.

Between Grant and Wood, rode Constables Chalmers and Young, two of Wood's handpicked men. Young exchanged a glance with Chalmers. The older constable's expression was grim as he looked uphill. The steep cliffs on either side of the trail seemed to close in on them like prison walls, the sharp rocks reaching up towards the rain-soaked clouds above.

"I'm not sure this rain's ever going to let up," Chalmers muttered, his voice cutting through the dull noise of the wind and rain. He glanced up at the clouds as they rolled over the mountains above them, thick and dark with the promise of more bad weather. "Feels like it's been coming down for weeks now."

Young grunted in agreement, his head down as he focused on guiding his horse over the slippery trail. "I've never seen it this bad so early in the year," he said, his voice low but tinged with concern. "We're going to be slogging through this mess all the way to the summit if the weather doesn't break."

"Best we can do is keep moving," Chalmers muttered.

"I wouldn't hold my breath for it to get any easier," Young replied, his voice hoarse from the damp. He looked over his shoulder, his eyes flicking briefly to Grant behind them.

"Isn't that always the way?" Chalmers said with a grim laugh, though it wasn't really a laugh at all. "It gets harder the closer you come to the end."

"I don't think we're anywhere near the end," Young grunted.

A crack of thunder sounded in the distance, its echo reverberating across the peaks.

"Grant, you're awful quiet back there," Young called out. "Everything alright?"

"If being soaked through to the skin and cold is alright? Then, yes. Just peachy Young."

Chalmers chimed in, and asked with a half-grin, "Are you and the Inspector going to keep glaring at each other the whole trip?"

Grant didn't answer immediately, his gaze never leaving Wood's back. "I'm just doing what needs to be done," he muttered in reply, as much as observation to himself as it was a reply to Chalmers.

Chalmers looked at him, eyebrow raised. "That's not what I asked. You and Wood have been at odds since we left Bennett. It shows through pretty clear, you know?"

"I know. What does it matter to you?" Grant fired back, perhaps a touch more hash than he intended.

Chalmers shrugged, unaffected by the sharpness of the response. "Just saying, Grant. Doesn't help any of us if you two can't get on the same page. We're not exactly in a position to afford a falling-out."

Grant knew Chalmers was right. This was no time for petty bickering, but he couldn't help the frustration bubbling up inside him. The risk of the mission was too great to be distracted by personal conflicts, but it was hard to let go of the feeling that Wood was questioning his ability, his judgment. After all, Grant had fought with Soapy Smith's gang before. He knew better than any of them what that outlaw type was capable of. He wasn't just some green recruit fresh off the trail. Wood, with his polished airs and sharp-eyed suspicion didn't seem to see it that way and it grated at Grant, deep into the very core of his being.

"Any advice on how to handle your boss?" Grant asked.

"He's not the kind of man who wears his heart on his sleeve," Chalmers observed, eyes flicking to the sky as another burst of wind and rain hit them. “The man’s been through a lot. People think because he’s got the rank that it’s smooth sailing for him, but it’s not. He’s had his own fair share of issues with the brass, and his loyalty, his real loyalty, is to the work. To the job. Not to a higher-up or to any political nonsense.”

“He sure has got it in for me,” Grant offered.

Chalmers chuckled softly, though there was no humour in the sound. “Trust doesn’t come easy for Wood. If you haven’t worked alongside him before, he won’t be subtle about not trusting you.”

Grant snorted, “That much I’ve gathered.”

Chalmers hesitated for a second, clearly measuring his words. "It’s not that complicated. He doesn’t see everything as black and white like the rest of us. If he thinks something could jeopardize his mission, or his men, he’ll go after it like a dog on a rabbit. With everything on the line, he sees you as a potential threat. Doesn’t matter that you’ve tangled with this gang before. Doesn’t matter that you’re experienced. To him? You’re unpredictable.”

“Unpredictable,” Grant repeated, frowning as he processed the word. “You make it sound like I’m a liability.”

“Not exactly,” Chalmers replied. “You’re more like a loose cannon. He doesn’t do well with unpredictability. Never has. He’s the type of man who likes to have everything in his control, everything planned. When you made that rumour about him getting recalled, you threw him off balance. He doesn’t like being thrown off balance.”

“Alright, I take your point,” Grant replied and bit his lip in frustration.

Chalmers shrugged, “Not much you can do except play by his rules for a bit. If you want to get the job done, you’ll need to figure out what makes him tick. Be patient with him. He’ll respect you more if you do that. You might even end up getting along better in the end.”

Grant shook his head in disbelief, “Patience. That’s what I need with Wood?”

“Yep,” Chalmers said, his tone very matter of fact. “It’s the only way to handle him. The thing about Wood is, he’s fiercely loyal. Once you get on his good side and prove that you’re all in, he'll back you up without question. But until then, you're walking a tightrope."

Grant wasn't sure what to make of that, but he felt there was truth in the Constable's advice. He had never been one to sit back and let others call the shots, but maybe, just maybe, Chalmers was right. If he wanted this mission to succeed, he would have to swallow his pride and play the part. For the good of the group, for the gold, and for whatever future this damn operation might bring to the territory.

Chalmers, as if sensing the change in Grant's mood, added, "For what it's worth? I think you've got what it takes. But don't let Wood's cold exterior fool you. He's not a bad man. He's just a hard one to get through to."

Grant gave a nod, "Thanks, I'll keep that in mind." He urged his horse Sophie forwards and climbed towards the front of their small queue.

As he approached Wood, the Inspector's back was straight, his shoulders squared, as though every ounce of his focus was being directed into their forward progress. Grant hated to admit it, but Wood had a way of commanding respect. Even with the tension that hung between them, Grant couldn't help but notice the effortless way Wood moved, as if the weather and the rugged trail didn't bother him at all.

Hearing the approaching horse behind him, Wood glanced over his shoulder. Meeting Grant's gaze for a moment, the distance between them remained.

"Getting bored of bringing up the rear, Constable?" Wood called out, his voice carrying above the wind. There was no malice in the words, but the underlying edge was unmistakable.

"Maybe so," Grant replied. "I thought we should address the unease between us."

"Is that so?" Wood replied, with an edge to his question.

"I realize that we haven't gotten off on the right foot. I admit, I should have spoken to you about my plan first. That was a mistake."

"You impugned my reputation on a whim," Wood said, his words slow and measured. "Rumour or not, that story will stick to my name."

“I apologize, Inspector.”

“I appreciate the apology,” Wood said finally, his voice softer but still edged with tension. “You don’t have to like me, but I do expect you to respect my position, even if you don’t agree with how I run things.”

"I respect you sir," Grant replied, his voice steady. “I’ll follow your lead, and I’ll watch you back. I expect the same.”

Wood didn’t respond right away, his gaze turning back to the path ahead. After a long pause, Wood said, “Don’t mistake me, Grant, I may not agree with your methods, but that doesn’t mean I don’t believe you’re capable for the dangers ahead. Whatever those may be. We’ll just have to see how this all plays out. Just don’t make me regret it.”

As the two men continued up the trail, their horses moved in near unison through the landscape. The climb continued in silence, the only sound the steady plodding of horses through the mud and the relentless rain pounding against the earth. Here, in the midst of it all, Grant had found a small sliver of clarity. Perhaps he didn’t have to fight Wood every step of the way. Maybe, all he had to do was prove that his actions, however rash they seemed, were for the greater good.

CHAPTER VII

The First Attempt

The rain had stopped. It wasn't the sort of break that promised sunshine and calm, but rather, a temporary cessation, as though nature had simply tired of its own downpour. When the clouds parted just enough to let the pale light of the late afternoon through, the air remained heavy with the sharp, biting chill of the lingering damp. The trees, their needles dripping with moisture, glistened in the fading daylight as the damp smell of wet pine and spruce filled the air.

The team had passed through the boreal forests and were now venturing towards the high alpine region of the Chilkoot as they arrived at Deep Lake. Like the pause in the continual rain, the Mounties took some solace in the fact that the climb would not be as continually steep anymore. However, the Chilkoot Pass itself still lay another eleven kilometres ahead of them. They would have to navigate rough alpine terrain, steep ridges, and winding paths through loose rock and tundra. Beyond the lake, they would leave the shelter of the trees, entering the stark open spaces of the highlands and cross back into the snowline. There was little time for rest, but the horses needed it. After they left here, they would be pushing hard once again.

Riding at the head of the column, Wood raised his hand and called out to the others, "We'll stop here to rest and water the horses."

Despite the misery of the weather, Grant had learned to appreciate the quiet camaraderie of this group. The familiar rhythm of the journey helped ease his mind, despite the twisting knots he had been feeling in his gut. Every so often, his hand would drift to his side, checking the dunnage bag behind his saddle, just one in their collection of heavy bags containing the gold and precious customs duties.

The spot Wood had chosen was a good one. It was a natural place for the horses to rest, where the water was clear and the ground slightly firmer. It was a few hundred metres away from a large tent and stockade camp, which were the local horse freighters. Orr and Tukey, out of Montana, transported the Stampeder's equipment from below the Chilkoot summit down to Lindeman or Bennett. For those who could afford their services, the horse, mule and jackass trains were a blessing after the climb and hauling required to get to the Canadian border. Grant had heard about the new aerial tramways that had been built to carry the equipment over the mountains. He was intrigued and curious to see these new technological marvels. How the first Stampeders had managed to carry everything on their backs in the first year, he could not contemplate, only offer his silent respect and admiration for the feats of those 'old timers'.

The Orr and Tukey camp was quiet when they arrived. Grant checked his brass pocket watch, it was midday. With a click he snapped its case shut and returned it to the pocket inside his jacket. He reckoned that all the teams must be out hauling and earning right now. They would likely cross paths with them later as their long train made its way back from the Pass. Now that the ice on the lakes had broken in the spring thaw, he wondered how much more difficult their days must have become. *Hauling, it must be a hard life*, he thought.

Sophie, Grant's horse, nickered softly as he loosened the saddle, allowing her a brief respite from the load and climb thus far. All the Mounties' horses were now eagerly drinking from the lake, their breath steaming up from their nostrils in the cool air.

Stood at the water's edge, Grant looked out over the pristine lake. The world around them felt so isolated here. Beyond the thick canopy of trees, it was quiet, the kind of quiet that made you feel exposed. The eerie stillness was almost unnatural. He'd seen changes in the landscape before as he had travelled the country, but this felt different to him. Here, in this place, it seemed they were about to enter a new, more dangerous phase of the journey.

"There's nothing quite like it," Grant muttered to himself, rubbing his hand over the thick scar on his left cheek.

"Don't like what?" the nearby Chalmers asked after hearing Grant's muttering.

"The quiet. The land. There's nothing quite like it," Grant said, squinting past the far edge of the lake, where the terrain began to rise towards the distant summit.

Chalmers expression was uncertain, "Feels too quiet. The air's too still for my taste. Give me a busy town any day of the week."

Grant nodded in agreement but remained lost in thought. As he stood there, looking at the looming mountains above and the stillness of the lake ahead, a deep sense of unease crept over him. It began as a prickle, a tingle, creeping along his spine. At the outer limits of his perception, he heard something faint and rhythmic. Almost imperceptible, he couldn't place it a first, but then awareness dawned as the sound grew closer. Hooves.

Not just one or two, but a group. Several horses at least. The beat was steady, measured. Thus far, they had not encountered any other groups travelling west. All the people they had passed were heading towards Lindeman or Bennett. All of them had been burdened with supplies and equipment that clanked, jangled and made a distinct travelling sound. Now, he could only hear hooves.

To his left, and closer to the trail they had left, Wood and Thompson were checking the supplies and double-checking the dunnage bags. Their movements were purposeful, but Grant noticed tension simmering between them. Wood was still the stiff, rigid Inspector, his focus always on the mission, asking the younger Constable a series of rapid-fire questions. Thompson appeared quieter now, no longer full of his usual boisterous energy as he answered. Was Wood's trust issues with anyone new being repeated here? Grant suspected that might be the case. *Thank you, Chalmers for your unsolicited insights*, Grant thought to himself.

Grant slipped his 1876 Winchester repeater carbine out of its saddle mounted scabbard. He checked its breech despite knowing a round was already chambered. He hefted the rifle and found its weight was a comfort in his hand.

Chalmers, always the practical one, asked, "What is it?"

Grant nodded back towards the trail, “Someone’s coming. Keep your eyes open.”

Chalmers turned from the lake and cocked his head to one side. “I hear them,” he said. “I told you it was too quiet.”

As Chalmers reached for his rifle, Grant took this opportunity to check on Thompson. Wood had left the younger Constable to go question Young about something else.

“Was Wood chewing your ear off?” Grant enquired.

“I’ve had worse,” Thompson replied as he tightened the saddle on his horse. He then moved to inspect the dunnage bags.

“Are you talking about me?” Grant fired back.

“No, Strickland.” He replied and laughed. “You’re not as bad as you think.”

Grant peered over Thompson’s shoulder and for the first time saw the group of approaching riders. What he saw confirmed what his ears had suggested, they weren’t hauling supplies, like the usual freighters or prospectors. They were travelling light there wasn’t any clanking of tools or equipment. Just the riders, focused, determined and armed. Were they following them?

“We’ve got company,” Grant told Thompson.

“Hey?” Thompson asked, and as he spoke the buckle that he had been pulling on failed. When it separated from the bag, the brass buckle fell and landed one side up in the mud below.

“Great quality,” Grant observed and bent down to collect the broken buckle.

A noise that didn’t belong in the wilderness followed. A crack was followed by a low whistle, a snap, and the thudding wet sound of metal hitting flesh.

Grant felt a wet splatter rain down across the back of his head and neck.

Next to the buckle, still stuck upright in the mud, fell Thompson’s torso. What remained of his head collapsed to the ground with a wet thud and final spray of arterial blood. As Grant stared into the maw of its horror, the abyss looked back at him in that moment, and it winked.

The riders had fired on them without warning. Time sped up once again and the world became a blur of action and noise.

Thompson's horse, splattered with blood and brain, screamed, then reared in surprise. The animal was about to bolt. Grant dropped his rifle, then managed stand and grab at the dangling reins. It was pure instinct as he yanked hard on the reins, hoping to regain a semblance of control. Doing so, he turned the horse towards and around him.

Another pair of shots rang out as the horse wheeled itself around, covering Grant's back. The shots both landed true, and the horse took the hammer blows from both bullets. The animal screamed again as it crashed to the ground near the shallows of the lake's shore.

"Ambush!" Grant heard Wood shout out, who then ordered the other all to, "Get down!"

Grant dropped behind the cover of the dead horse and pressed his back against its still warm body. He could feel more shots thudding home into its back. His rifle was laying in the mud nearby, agonizingly just out of reach. When he had tried to reach out, shots hit the ground beside it, sending up sprays of dirt and debris. Grant drew his Adams revolver from its holster and peered over the horse's now still body.

There were at least half a dozen men waiting at the tree line, about thirty metres away, rifles raised and pouring their concentrated fire into Thompson's dead horse. A bullet slammed home into the horse's flank closest to his head. He was pinned down. Grant ducked, his heart pounding in his chest as shot after shot hit the horse's carcass.

From somewhere beyond the trees, a wavering voice called out, "Grant! Don't make this harder than needs be!"

Then came the pounding of hooves.

Grant took a breath and looked over the carcass again. Two riders had peeled away from the tree line, spurring their horses straight toward his cover. One had their revolver out, snapping off wild shots, while the other brandished a long hunting knife, his lips peeled back in a snarl.

Grant didn't hesitate. He popped up and fired twice. Both shots punched through the lead rider's chest, sending him spilling sideways out of the saddle to the ground. The second man veered around the other's horse and vaulted from the saddle, knife flashing downwards as he lunged.

Grant barely had time to roll aside as the blade slashed down, just catching outer layer of his coat's heavy fabric. He twisted, bringing his gun up, but the man was too close now. A fist cracked against Grant's jaw, knocking him back against the carcass of the horse. Stars burst in his vision. Before he could recover, a boot kicked him hard in the ribs, and he gasped in pain.

"Die, Mountie," the man snarled.

Grant shook his head, spitting blood from his split lip. The knife-wielding outlaw came at him again, but Grant was ready this time. He caught the man's wrist, twisting hard, forcing the blade away. With a sharp jab of his revolver, he struck the man in his throat. The strike drove the outlaw back just enough for Grant to level the gun and fire. One shot rang out, then the man crumpled to the mud, lifeless.

Breathing hard, Grant snatched up his rifle and ducked back behind the horse. He wiped at the blood on his lip. All he could smell was gunpowder and taste the coppery blood in his mouth.

A new flurry of gunfire erupted. The Mounties who had taken cover by the lakeshore now fired back towards the gang with directed precision. Grant took the opportunity to peer over the horse again to gauge the state of their attackers.

The riders had dismounted before the lakeshore, and each outlaw had moved quickly to take cover behind the trees and large rocks that lined the edges of the trail. They had fanned out and were attacking from cover, hoping to force the Mounties to expose themselves. Their leader, presumably, was the one still on horseback, barking orders and directing the gang. From his elevated position, he had a clear view of the battlefield. He was being cautious.

Grant recognized the man's voice; he was the one who had just called out to him. *Who was he?* Grant thought. When the man turned his horse once more, he got a better look at the leader's face. It was familiar. He was one of McCade's men who had taken him hostage some months back. Grant cast his memory back and recalled the man but not his name.

As if on cue, he heard another one of the outlaw's voices ring out from the tree line, "Damn it, Milton. Quit pissing about and let's get this done!"

Milton.

The name now echoed in Grant's mind, a dark realization flooding over him. One of Soapy Smith's hired guns. The realization struck hard, but Grant didn't have time to dwell on it.

When the last of McCade's men had surrendered at White Pass, Milton wasn't among them. Grant had assumed that Milton had been killed either in Lillian's dynamite driven ambush, or in the avalanche they had caused later. Obviously, he had been wrong. The gunfire intensified, and Grant's world narrowed to a pinpoint of focus: survival. His breath came in shallow gasps as he pushed himself to his knees. He returned fire, aiming for their attackers. He didn't care who they were or why they were here. All that mattered was keeping himself and the team alive.

Grant crouched low, looking for a way to break the stalemate. He couldn't stay hidden behind this dead horses forever. The Mounties had to make a move. But these outlaws weren't going to give up any opening. Every time one of the Mounties tried to peek around cover, a shot rang out, forcing them back. Grant's eyes locked onto Milton. The outlaw leader wasn't reckless, but he wasn't pressing home the advantage of surprise either.

"Grant!" Wood shouted from behind the cover of a large rock. "They're targeting you!"

Grant's breath caught for a moment. Of course! They weren't there for the gold, he had been the target from the start. Milton had come for him. This was revenge.

Another series of shots rang out.

"We're coming to you!" Wood called out as he, Chalmers and Young advanced from their position towards Grant. Chalmers and Young were firing their carbine repeaters in unison. Wood fired back, adding the crack of his revolver's shots to the deafening lakeside chaos.

Grant levelled his own rifle and took aim. The first man he targeted was Milton. As his eyes locked on, he saw the man's face was twisted in a cold, dangerous sneer. Milton's rifle was aimed directly at the advancing Mounties. He pulled the trigger, and that shot rang out loud and clear above all the others.

Young crumpled to the ground with a cry of pain.

"NO!" Chalmers screamed out.

Another shot thudded home into Young's chest.

"Young!" Chalmers called out, and his words were filled with anguish. There was no time to mourn. The gunfire hadn't stopped. The outlaws were eager to finish what they had started.

Grant was on his feet in an instant. Moving to one side, he fired and racked the weapon's action; fired; racked; fired; racked and fired again. One man went down, and another staggered back, clutching his leg. But the cost had already been paid. The death of a Constable was always the highest price to pay, but two in the blink of an eye? Grant knew they couldn't lose anyone else. His blood boiled. This ambush wasn't a robbery, it was personal.

The shots continued to ring out. Chalmers' voice had cut through the noise, urgent, as he pulled Young out of the line of fire, but the Constable was already gone. He was dead, his body laying still as he was dragged through the muck towards a safety that was no longer possible.

Grant couldn't hold back the fury that surged inside him. He had to end this now; or they were all dead. He chambered another round and fired again; this time his shot caught the Outlaw next to Milton square in the heart. The outlaw's eyes widened in shock as he fell backwards to the muddy earth.

His rifle now empty, with a roar of determination, Grant surged from cover, tossing the Winchester aside. He drew his revolver and aimed. In the blink of an eye, he fired, the bullet finding its mark, passing through Milton's nose into and through his brain. The outlaw dropped senseless from his saddle; the life had drained from his eyes before he even hit the ground.

The remaining attackers hesitated, then turned to flee. But they were too slow. The Mounties were on them in seconds, cutting them down one by one. Justice and revenge melded into one single action: ending those who had attacked them. The battle was over. Milton lay still in the mud, never to rise again.

When the gunfire finally stopped, silence fell over the scene. The only sound now was the ragged breathing of the survivors.

Grant stood still for a moment, his chest heaving as the adrenaline drained from his body. His hand trembled as he holstered his revolver. His eyes locked on the fallen bodies of his comrades. Young and Thompson were dead, killed in the line of duty. Too many lives lost in an ambush that should never have happened.

"Damn it," Grant muttered under his breath.

Wood, his face pale and strained, looked over at Grant, his expression hard.

"We have to keep moving," Wood said quietly, his voice heavy with the weight of their losses. "We can't stop. Not now."

Grant didn't respond. He couldn't. The loss of two good men was too fresh, too raw. He nodded; his jaw clenched. He didn't speak. There was nothing left to say.

The road to Skagway had just become that much darker. The mission was still on, but it had cost them dearly.

CHAPTER VIII

Crater Lake

The wind had teeth at this altitude, biting through layers of wool and fur-lined coats to find any available gap in a man's clothing. Once they reached the snowline, the Mounties had broken out their Buffalo coats. Just like at White Pass, spring had not yet crept its way into these elevations.

Grant hunched deeper under his raised collar as he, Chalmers and Wood carefully guided their small train of four horses to step around discarded supplies and half-buried debris. Their boots crunched against the hard packed snow and ice, and behind them, the still frozen Crater Lake reflected the weak light of late afternoon. The well packed snow of the debris field steered them directly to the terminus of the aerial tramway and the chute that lead up towards the Chilkoot's summit.

They could hear the operation before they saw it, the deep groan of pulleys straining under heavy loads, the metallic grind of the cables, and the occasional sharp clack as the rectangular cars launched over the chute returned to the earth as they landed near the lake's edge and the tramway's endpoint, known as Stone Crib.

At the top of the chute, high above the frozen basin around Crater Lake, a series of wooden A-frame towers loomed against the overcast grey sky, with broad crossbeams that splayed out their cables. The Chilkoot Railroad & Transport Company's aerial tramway's sets of steel wire wrapped cables swung the cargo over the Pass and down to the lakeside terminus. Considering the volume of materials being unloaded, it appeared that most Stampeders seemed more than happy to pay the company's fees rather than risk carrying their burdens down from the pass themselves. Business was brisk as sleds, crates, barrels, and canvas-wrapped bundles were being unloaded from the cars and baskets, then shunted along wooden platforms, stacked and stored, waiting for their turn to be loaded onto the horses and mules of the freighter companies that worked the circuit from here to Lindeman City or Bennett Lake.

As Grant had expected, the Mounties passed the main train of pack animals making their return journey from Stone Crib. 'Fleet' seemed to be a more accurate description, for Grant, than 'train' as it must have easily been a group of well over a hundred animals. Led by a single horse, a bell around its neck, the fleet was supervised by a team of wranglers.

After the attack at Deep Lake, the team were suspicious of every group that approached them, their fingers ready by the triggers of their rifles. Once the enormous herd had continued to placidly pass them by, they relaxed and had watched the mass of materials being moved with efficiency and purpose.

Below the tramway's towers, the chute itself was a carved-out groove in the ice that plunged a few hundred metres straight down the slope from the summit. The Stampeders who had not taken advantage of this tramway's service had to navigate this short, sharp descent with their supplies. The steep, treacherous route was lined with travellers, their breath rising in thick clouds. One full sled broke away from its owner's control and rocketed downhill at dangerous speed. The men at the bottom of the chute scrambled to avoid the missile. As the sled hit a bank of snow at the bottom, it flipped, sending packs and provisions flying.

Wood chuckled, "Hell of a system." He reined in his horse near the periphery of the staging area, looked up towards the tramway, and said, "However, that: is a hell of a thing."

Grant agreed, and added, "A wonder of our modern age."

The Mounties trudged closer to the tramway's terminus, their horses' breath steaming in the cold. They had spent so long looking over their shoulders after the attack that the normal bustle of frontier life almost felt foreign. However, the impact of what had happened hadn't lessened. Grant's eyes scanned the area, taking in the groups of Stampeders gathered at the lake's frozen edge, preparing for the next leg of their journey. So many faces, so much movement. It was impossible to tell if they were being watched. That made him uneasy. His mind remained stuck on the attack, on the gunfire, on the bodies of Thompson and Young.

They had been forced to leave their dead behind. That thought sat heavy in his chest.

Wood, it seemed, had picked up on Grant's ruminations. He asked him, "You're still at Deep Lake, aren't you?"

Grant pulled his coat tighter against the cold, "Hard not to be."

"Chalmers, check in with whoever's running this place. Find out about how we best to get up to the summit. We'll wait here."

"Sir," Chalmers replied and tied off his horse to an abandoned sled.

Wood followed suit as Chalmers left in search of the foreman. Wood brushed the snow off a nearby crate before sitting. He sighed as he rubbed the stiffness from his legs.

"It was all too fast."

Grant answered, "I should be dead."

"That's nonsense," Wood replied.

"Thompson's dead. Young's dead. If they'd come at us any harder, I'd be dead, too." Grant tightened his grip on the reins. "For what? Because some coward like Milton wanted me gone?"

Wood didn't argue. He just sat there, watching the men unloading another tramway basket. The growing pile of cargo was becoming more chaotic with each load and the handlers were struggling to keep up with the tide. A barrel slipped free and rolled across the hard packed icy ground, nearly taking out one of them. Someone cursed, and laughter rose from the onlookers.

Nearby, a wiry man in a fur-lined coat barked, "Keep it steady, damn you! Don't just let go! Ease it!"

Wood watched as Chalmers approached the man, before he said to Grant, "We all could be dead. This Milton? He was after you, specifically. Do you think it was revenge for White Pass?"

"What else could it be? When I was their prisoner, I barely had any interaction with Milton. I wouldn't have thought he'd be so keen to avenge McCade's death, but what do I know?"

"Perhaps it was someone else who wanted revenge?"

"Soapy Smith?" Grant replied with a snort. "If Soapy had sent him he'd have come with thirty men to take the money."

"Perhaps he doesn't know about the money yet," Wood surmised. "Perhaps, he just wants you dead."

"Perhaps," Grant murmured, unconvinced.

"At this point, guilt doesn't serve anyone but the enemy," Wood said. He then further instructed Grant, "I need you present, not preoccupied with beating yourself up over everything little thing that's outside of your control."

Grant didn't answer right away. He focused on the flow of men working around them, the tide of hopefuls and hired hands, all pushing north towards Lindeman City and Bennett. The attack on their group had been a violent reminder that not everyone would survive the frontier. Some would die on the trail. Some poor fools wouldn't last until the winter. Others would die fighting for a fortune they had only dreamed of and hadn't yet won. He sighed, Wood was right, he needed to be focused on the present and the task at hand.

"You're right. Leaving them behind felt wrong. It doesn't sit well with me," admitted Grant.

"Orr and Tukey Freight will bring them back to Bennett. There's nothing else we could do. The mission comes first. They knew that. They would understand."

Grant nodded but didn't answer.

"They won't be forgotten," Wood added.

Grant turned to him, his jaw tight. "It won't bring them back though."

"No, it won't," agreed Wood.

The wind picked up, sending a fresh gust of snow swirling around them. The tramway groaned under another load, its pulleys creaked. The conversation was interrupted by the crunch of boots on the packed snow as Chalmers returned from the tramway, along with another Constable.

"Foreperson's a right bastard," he announced, rubbing his hands together for warmth. "We'll have to leave the horses here. The chute's too slick for them. This is Constable Henry."

"Inspector," Henry greeted Wood and saluted.

"Easy Henry, that's not required." Wood replied with a wave of his hand, then asked, "What's the procedure for getting to the summit?"

"Feet, sir. It's a climb. There's no room for horses up top, you'll see."

"What about the tramway?" Grant asked.

"This one doesn't stop at the summit, it goes clear over to Sheep Camp on the Alaskan side," Henry answered. "Seven cents per pound."

Wood frowned, "That's a problem."

Chalmers shrugged. "No way around it. It's either that or we haul it up ourselves."

Grant didn't say anything. He could already see the tension in Wood's face.

Their baggage wasn't just bedrolls and provisions. It was a nearly two hundred thousand dollars in gold, coin and banknotes. It was more than the three men could carry by themselves.

Wood's jaw tightened. "I don't like the idea of it being out of our sight."

"Neither do I," agreed Grant. "We don't have much of a choice. The tram's the only way over."

They turned to watch as another uncontrolled sled came roaring down the chute, nearly flipping at a sharp bend before crashing into the pile below. More handlers ran forward, most shouting, some laughing.

Chalmers stamped his feet against the cold. "What's the call?"

Wood exhaled sharply, rubbing a hand over his chin. "One way or another, I have to check in with Inspector Belcher at the summit. We climb."

Chalmers raised an eyebrow, "Yes, sir."

Wood nodded at Chalmers, "You stay here with the baggage. Grant and I will go ahead, make sure there aren't any surprises waiting for us at the top."

Chalmers smirked. "You two, climbing that chute? Rather you than me."

"Constable Henry, I'll need you to stand guard with Chalmers here." Wood directed the new Constable. "Don't worry, I'll square it all away with Belcher when I see him."

Grant glanced at the incline. It was going to be a hell of an ascent. But he'd rather suffer the climb than let the baggage out of their sight entirely.

"Let's move," Grant muttered.

"That's what I like to hear," Wood chuckled. "No rest for the wicked, this mountain isn't going to climb itself."

The wind picked up again as Wood and Grant started off toward the base of the chute and the icy ascent that lay ahead of them.

CHAPTER IX

The Summit

The merciless wind crossing the summit of Chilkoot Pass carried with it a stinging spray of fine snow that whipped against every exposed patch of skin. It sliced through the spaces between the stacked piles of freight and tramway towers with an unrelenting howl. The summit was less a wilderness and more of an overburdened depot, a confusing crossroads where thousands of Stampeders' fortunes were balanced between perseverance and failure.

The Pass itself wasn't more than a hundred-yard-wide trench between two peaks that loomed a further five-hundred feet above the frozen chaotic jumble of men and heaped cargo crates, barrels, and canvas-wrapped bundles. A tattered Union Jack fluttered in the wind above the small wooden cabin at its centre. When the weather was clear, one could see all the way to Dyea and the unending line of Stampeders approaching from the town. Today, the sky hung low and grey, obscuring any view beyond the summit.

Sets of tramway cables cut through the landscape. The skeletal wooden framework of their towers was coated thick with frost. The runs of steel wrapped cables were stretched taut against the sky, creaking under the weight of their loads. Massive sledges, buckets and cargo cars, heavy with provisions, swung in the wind as they ascended from The Scales, a basin north of Sheep Camp, some twenty-five-hundred feet below them on the Alaskan side of the Coastal Mountains.

The cables of the CR&T tramway swung their loads high above the rest, on their non-stop journeys from Sheep Camp across the border to Crater Lake and back again. The terminus of the other tramways were here, at the summit's periphery, disgorging their contents with a repetitive tedium. Each load was another man's chance at surviving the brutal march to Dawson and their stay thereafter. The summit was a city of freight, a frozen bottleneck of commerce, ambition and exhaustion and the tramways had become its arteries.

The wooden unloading station was a makeshift structure, built from rough-hewn logs and reinforced with iron bolts to withstand the brutal mountain winds. A narrow walkway, covered in a thin sheet of ice, extended out toward the cable where workers in heavy wool coats and fur-lined hats waited with hooks and crowbars, then scrambled to unload the gear from the cars that arrived steadily minute after minute.

"Coming in!" a tram operator shouted over the wind, signalling his crew to be ready for the next car.

The cargo car arrived with a metallic groan, the steel clips screeching as they hit the braking mechanism. This car was nothing more than a wooden platform reinforced with metal brackets, but it carried an immense load: a mound of canvas wrapped provisions strapped down with thick ropes. The weight of the shipment forced the entire platform to dip for a moment before it settled into place.

Two men rushed forward with long iron poles, jamming them into hooks along the side to keep the load steady. A third worker yanked free the locking pin, releasing the car from the tram cable. It hit the unloading dock with a heavy thud, sending a fine spray of snow into the air.

Another tram worker grabbed a thick iron hook and leaned in, his breath a cloud of frost as he worked the latch free. The steel cables snapped back, recoiling with a sudden jolt.

"Unclipped!" one of the workers barked.

Wood and Grant watched as a team of four men rushed forward, grabbing the heavy ropes tied around the cargo. They grunted under the weight, dragging it across the ice-slicked platform toward the ever-growing pile of supplies that dominated the summit.

Grant exhaled sharply, "This is worse than White Pass."

Wood nodded, “It’s a miracle anything gets through.”

“And that everyone still has all their toes,” added Grant.

Crates, barrels, sacks, and bundles were stacked high in haphazard rows, some completely buried under snow and ice. Wooden boxes marked with the chalked last names of their owners and rough descriptions like ‘Flour,’ ‘Salt Pork,’ ‘Beans,’ and ‘Whiskey’ were piled alongside wool blankets, tools or even canoes. Large barrels, likely filled with lard, molasses, or salted fish, sat frozen in the snow, their lids crusted over with ice.

Between these towering stacks, narrow passageways had formed, creating a network of snowy corridors where Stampeders huddled in makeshift shelters, waiting their turn to claim their goods. Some men paced nervously, while others sat on their own crates, chewing hard biscuits and blowing into their hands for warmth. The scents of sweat, damp wool, and frozen leather clung to the air, barely masked by the occasional whiff of burning wood from a distant campfire, creating an aroma that was both familiar and unpleasant to the Mounties.

At the far end of the tramway station, another empty car was hooked onto the downward cable, ready for its return down to The Scales. A tram operator cranked the winch, releasing the brake with a metallic *clank*. The empty car lurched forward, tilted sharply, then picked up speed as it disappeared down the slope, swallowed whole by the swirling snow.

“Line’s been running steady all morning,” a tram worker muttered to their colleague as the pair walked past Wood and Grant, their boots leaving deep prints in the snow. “Storm comes in, though? The whole damn thing will seize up again.”

“Same day, same shit pay,” his colleague growled in reply.

Grant studied the grey overcast sky, “We should get on the move,” he murmured.

As Wood and Grant trudged away from their view of the tram station, their boots crunched on the packed ice beneath them. Amassed around the small wood cabin at the centre of the Pass, sleds, packed high with supplies, waited in long, disordered rows, their owners either securing permits or haggling over the customs duties with the red-coated Constables. The cabin stood like a small island in this storm of humanity, a wooden shack reinforced with rough-cut logs, its roof bowed under the weight of the snowdrifts that had virtually buried it.

Several tents were pitched around the cabin, and a Constable was busy shovelling off the fresh snow that had accumulated on them before the canvas and wood structures collapsed. Beside the tents sat the veiled menace of the outpost's Maxim gun position, ready to bark and deal out death should any Stampeders choose to act the fool.

Grant pointed it out as they passed, "I see they have one too."

"Yes, the devil's own paintbrush," Wood replied.

Inside the cramped cabin, the warmth was immediate, as was a distinct, uncomfortable dampness. Regardless, it was a welcome contrast to the cutting cold outside. A wood stove crackled in the corner, the scent of burning spruce thick in the room. A buffalo coat and a Biltmore Stetson, stiff with frost, were draped over chair near the heat, steaming as they thawed.

Inspector Belcher sat behind a hodgepodge structure of a desk, made of discarded shipping crates and a broken sled. He was studying a handwritten manifest by the dim glow of an oil lamp. His uniform, though neat and ordered, looked worn, the wool dulled from exposure to the extremes of the mountain climate.

Without looking up, he spoke. "Any disputes are handled by the Constables outside. Not by me."

Wood pulled off his gloves, shaking out his numbed fingers, "Inspector Wood and Constable Grant."

Belcher grunted and lifted his gaze, his steel-grey eyes scanning them both. "I was told to expect your arrival. How was your journey?"

Grant gave a small nod, "We lost two men."

Belcher's face remained unreadable behind his broad moustache. "And your cargo?"

"Intact," Wood replied.

Belcher studied them for a moment longer, "Was it natural circumstances or by interference?"

"Interference," Wood replied. "We were attacked near Deep Lake."

"Damned unfortunate," Belcher observed. "Sit down before you fall down."

Wood and Grant shrugged off their heavy coats and took seats on two rough wooden chairs across from the makeshift desk. Grant stretched his legs, feeling the ache in his knees from the climb.

Belcher's brow furrowed. "It was an ambush?"

Grant nodded grimly. "Eight of them. They must have been following our trail. They came up hard with no warning."

Belcher rubbed a hand over his face. "Who were they?"

Grant glanced at Wood, then answered "I recognized one of them. Milton. An outlaw who used to ride with a gang out of Skagway."

Belcher scowled, "Soapy Smith's lot?"

Wood nodded his head. "That's the one. This Milton was after Grant here. He helped stop that attack on White Pass."

Belcher swore under his breath and leaned forward, elbows on the desk. "Indeed? I've heard about you, Grant. Well done."

"I did what I had to," Grant replied, dismissing the praise.

"If I've heard of you then Soapy Smith has heard of you. White Pass put you on someone's bad side. Men lost gold, lost friends. If this Milton was there for payback, that worries me. If someone has put a price on your head, you can bet they won't stop after one failed attempt."

Wood nodded. "All the more reason why we shouldn't stay up here longer than we have to."

"Best you get under way sooner rather than later. You can take that off my hands as well." Belcher pointed towards his humble cot.

Underneath, barely visible in the dim light of the shack, lay a heavy canvas bag.

"Stuffed with coins and notes. I'll be happy to see it go."

Grant eyed the bag. "Hell of a place to keep it."

"Safer than any bank," Belcher replied. He chuckled, it was a wet, gurgling sound that became a series of hacking coughs. After clearing the phlegm, Belcher let out a tired sigh and rubbed his hands together. "It does help pay the heating costs though. Damn cold up here." He nodded toward the small cast-iron stove in the corner, where a thin stream of smoke curled from the stovepipe. "That little beast's hunger is the most expensive thing in this shack. Do you know how much wood is going for up here? Just over a dollar a pound. Likely reach two before the thaw comes."

Grant let out a low whistle. "Hell, you can buy a hot meal in Bennett for that."

Belcher grunted and took another sip of coffee. "It's not just that, every log, every split stick we burn is hauled in by sled from miles off. Stampeders don't think about that when they're trudging through waist-high snow, but up here? Firewood is gold."

"Speaking of which," Wood interjected. "Any suggestion for how we get it all down the mountain? Ours is still down at Crater Lake. My man Chalmers is guarding it with one of yours, Constable Henry."

"Henry's a good enough sort. Not exactly the sharpest of knives, but at least he's not corrupt," Belcher said, he paused considering Wood's question. "I'd suggest the tramway is your most direct route."

"I'm not too keen on it travelling unprotected." Wood replied.

"I understand, the longer you're out in the open, the more vulnerable you are. The trams are the fastest way to get across. I can guarantee no one is going to touch the cargo when it's swinging three hundred feet overhead. I'd suggest one of you travels with it and the rest meet them down at Sheep Camp."

"Not the worst idea," Wood said as he pondered the scenario. "It cuts out the risks of the descent."

"It would be a shame to lose it all in an avalanche," Belcher added. "We had several back in April. Killed scores of men."

"What about us?"

"We're disposable as the next man," Belcher rebuffed Grant. He looked towards Wood and added, "To that end, you'll need another gun on the way down. I'll lend you Sergeant Pringle."

Wood hesitated. "You sure you can spare him?"

Belcher gave a wry smile. "Hardly. But I'd rather loan you a man than explain why I didn't help protect a quarter-million dollars' worth of customs money. That means trouble."

Wood gave a slow nod. "I appreciate it. We'll take him."

Belcher smirked, "Pringle's steady. He won't let you down."

Belcher leaned back, studying them for a moment. "You'll need dog sleds or horses once you're stateside."

Grant smirked, "That shouldn't be an issue, we're got enough funds to pay for the help."

"There's a musher down at Sheep Camp, goes by Draper. He's honest, but don't let anyone know what you're carrying," Belcher warned them. "If Soapy Smith finds out what you're hauling, you'll be dead before you hit tidewater. If anyone tries to interfere again, well..." He tapped the holster on his hip, and said, "I trust you boys can handle yourselves."

Wood smirked. "That we do."

Belcher pushed himself back from the desk and stood. "Come with me."

Outside, the wind bit even harder as Belcher led them through the maze of goods and towards the tramway station.

Belcher gestured at the chaos around them.

"Every man here thinks he's bound for Dawson," he said, his voice carrying over the wind. "Every pile of gear you see belongs to someone trying to survive the winter up there. And most of them won't make it that far."

A figure stepped forward from the group of Constables who were inspecting a newly arrived series of cartes, Sergeant Pringle.

Pringle was a hard-faced man, broad-shouldered and built like an ox. His rifle was slung across his back, its stock worn smooth from years of use. The rifle's strap crisscrossed the bandolier of shells strapped across his barrel chest. He had the look of someone who had spent more time in the wilderness and too little time around soft company.

Belcher breezed through the introductions and got to his orders, "Sergeant Pringle, this is Inspector Wood and Constable Grant. You'll be assisting them."

Pringle gave a single nod. "Where are we headed?"

"Skagway," Wood answered.

"What they're carrying may attract some unwanted attention, Pringle. If that happens, you're to prevent any outside interference, with extreme prejudice."

Pringle gave Wood and Grant a once-over and said, "Sounds like my kind of assignment."

CHAPTER X

A Harrowing Descent

The morning air was sharp with the scent of frost and woodsmoke. Having spent a cold, but quiet night in some of the Chilkoot detachment's tents near the Stone Crib terminus of the tramway, Chalmers and Grant drank stale coffee out of battered tin mugs as they braced themselves for the day ahead.

Standing on the tram's wooden loading platform they were staring out at the cable lines that snaked above the chute, up and over the Chilkoot's summit. Tram cars hung like beads on its string, swaying slightly with the motion of the traction cable that groaned against the weight of the supplies heading towards them direct from Alaska. Snow and ice clung to the thick wooden beams supporting the tram towers, their heavy bracing sunk deep into the rock and frost. The steel cables hummed faintly as cargo cars appeared out of the mist that clung to the Chilkoot summit before they rattled their way down to the station. The entire contraption was a marvel of necessity. Dangerous, sure, but far better than breaking a man's back hauling cargo over the pass. They were resigned to leaving their horses behind, they would travel back to Bennett with the next horse fleet that came to Stone Crib. Grant had said goodbye to his mare Sophie earlier and was sad to leave her behind. He found himself surprised by the attachment he had grown to the stout Alberta Pony who had become his regular mount since he was seconded to the White Pass detachment.

A few workers moved between the Constables, their breath misting in the cold as they checked traction grips and the ranger arms that latched to the cars. Chalmers shifted uncomfortably beside Grant; his shoulders hunched against the cold. He eyed the two tramway cars ahead of them. They were glorified open air wooden platforms, with their collection of eight regulation canvas dunnage bags, a pair of heavy leather Gladstone bags, along with the team's saddle bags and effects were being strapped down to them by the tramway attendants. The car platforms hung below the trucks that would run them along the main cable.

His expression darkening, Chalmers muttered, "You sure about this, Grant?"

"Not even slightly," Grant chuckled and exhaled a breath of mist into the frigid air. "Unless you want to carry all of that on our backs, this is the best way."

Letting out a low grunt, Chalmers' expression made it clear he wasn't convinced. He'd seen the tramway in action but had never seen anyone ride it. Few men who had ever left the safety of the solid ground beneath their feet looked forward to dangling over a sheer drop held by nothing but a clasp on a steel wire.

"You've got to be joking," Chalmers muttered under his breath.

A station worker in a heavy wool coat and a fur-lined cap came up behind them. "You're all set," he said. "Cargo is secured, and you two will be riding separate." He jerked his chin toward the first tram car ahead of the others. It was a low wooden bucket, not more than three feet long, a few feet wide and deep.

"After you, Constable," the man said and waved Chalmers forward.

Chalmers asked Grant, "You trust this thing?"

"Enough," Grant answered. Then, after a moment, "Mostly."

"That's not what I wanted to hear," he groaned.

Chalmers hesitated for half a second too long. Grant smirked and clapped him on the shoulder. "You'll be fine."

Chalmers shot him a glare but didn't argue. His jaw worked as if he were chewing over his options, but in the end, he had none. With a stiff nod, he tossed his empty mug and stepped toward the bucket in front of their cargo's cars.

"Good man," Grant said, clapping him on the shoulder as he passed.

He stepped stiffly toward the tramway and climbed inside, gripping the bucket's wooden sides with white-knuckled hands as though they might suddenly vanish beneath him. As he eased himself down, the moment his weight settled, the tram car shifted with a faint jolt.

"If I die on this contraption, I will haunt you for the rest of your days," Chalmers said in farewell.

As the station crew latched the bucket's friction grip closed around the traction cable, it rose from the platform and with a jolt the bucket lurched forward, climbing into open space. Chalmers sucked in a sharp breath; his face paler than usual as he transferred his death grip from the sides of the bucket to its hanger arms that connected to the truck above him.

"Bloody hell," he barked.

As the tram workers connected the two cargo cars that would follow Chalmers, Grant stepped forward and settled himself down into another bucket like Chalmers did. That's when he began to feel a similar sense of dis-ease. The narrow bucket wasn't much more than a short and stubby coffin that didn't fit him. It was not built for emotional or physical comfort. Following Chalmer's example, Grant's gloved hands seized the bucket's hanger arms and waited for the moment when he too would be swung up from the solid earth and into an uncertain future in the sky.

"Give Alaska my regards," the attendant said as he threw the release lever forwards, engaging the friction grip.

The bucket lurched violently as it made purchase with the drive cable and left the platform, the steel cables groaning as it took up Grant's weight. His gloved hands stiff from the cold, he was certain he couldn't hold on with any more force than he was currently exerting. The first sensations were a slow, weightless glide as the car eased forward, then a sharper lurch as gravity took hold.

The wind caught at him immediately, sharp and biting as the tramway climbed. Grant inhaled deeply, adjusting to the steady sway of the car as it settled into its course. Looking back, Crater Lake shrank away, its frozen surface crisscrossed with the tracks of men and sleds hauling their gear toward the staging areas. The

Stone Crib was already becoming distant, the figures of the workers growing smaller against the endless white.

The cable creaked as the bucket passed the first support mast, the wooden beams of its A-frame braced against the wind and snow. The metal pulleys groaned above and the shift in weight caused the cables to vibrate with a low, thrumming hum. Grant felt the shift in weight as the bucket tipped backwards, angling into its ascent toward the summit.

Further ahead, Chalmers didn't move much. Grant could tell from the way he held himself, shoulders locked and head low, that he was gripping the sides of his car with everything he had.

Grant leaned back, it was an eerie sensation, moving without effort through the sky. When he glanced down, the ground was a sheer drop below with nothing but open air between him and the snow-covered rock face that was slipping rapidly away.

The wind changed direction, catching the tram cars and making them sway ever so slightly. Grant felt the pull in his gut, the instinctive bracing of a man who understood exactly how far he was from the ground.

As they crested the ridge above the chute, one by one their cars slipped into the mists swirling around the summit of the pass. For the next moments, they were enveloped by the mist and unable to see anything around them. They listened to the wind, the creak of the cables and the squealing of the wheels of the tramway's trucks as they were pulled towards Alaska.

When the mists broke, the summit was revealed, and Grant could see the border. The outpost's cluster of tents and stacked cargo lay half buried in the snow drifts. The Mounties' small cabin came into sight, the resilient, uncomfortable shelter where the red-coated lawmen monitored the Stampeders crossing into Canada. The smoke from its stovepipe chimney was whisked away by the strong wind, as the nearby Union Jack snapped and fluttered from its stumpy flagpole.

Beyond the cabin, Grant looked down at the terminus of two other tramways, those wooden towers and pulley systems marked where the Alaska Railroad & Transport and Dyea-Klondike Tramways offloaded their cargo. Steam rose from the Stampeders and sled teams gathered below, waiting to haul their freight down the chute to Crater Lake and beyond. A few figures moved along the platforms, bundled in their heavy buffalo coats and broad Biltmore Stetsons as they checked manifests and inspected baggage.

Ahead of Grant, the cars carrying the customs duties creaked as they swayed in their transit. The baggage was lashed down tight, but he knew better than to trust anything completely out here. It was a precious burden, more than a quarter of a million dollars in various forms, the weight of fortune itself. The irony wasn't lost on Grant. Here they were, carrying a small empire's worth of gold and currency, held in place by nothing more than a few ropes and the trust of steel cables.

Grant leaned against the side of his bucket, peering ahead. They had crossed the border, leaving the summit behind them. The wheels in the mechanism of his bucket's truck and the friction grip on the drive cable groaned as they passed one of the wooden support towers, the thick timber posts creaking against the strain. Grant watched the mechanism keeping tension on the cable. As the tram line tipped downwards toward Sheep Camp, he could feel the shift beneath him, the way the car adjusted to the angle. The engineers who built this system knew what they were doing, but still, it was an uncomfortable and unnatural feeling for Grant.

And then:

The descent.

The tramway didn't hesitate, it plunged downward along the steel cables, the weight of the cargo cars pushing against the drive cable, willing the cables to pull them faster. It was a near vertical drop flanked by ragged cliffs.

Grant swore violently as he gripped the sides of his bucket, feeling the vibration of the cables, his stomach tightened as the stone walls rushed past. Despite the terror, the view ahead was breathtaking. The wilderness of Alaska stretched before him, a world of ice and rock, wind; and, in the distance: green forests reaching to the sea. Snowdrifts clung to the passing ridges; loose powder swirled in ghostly wisps as the ever-present gales swept along the narrow corridor. Passing along the long span of cable, the panoramic, dynamic view kept Grant mesmerized until the bucket lurched again as it crossed the tower overlooking the Chilkoot's false summit and a new, sheer drop.

The infamous Golden Staircase was visible far below now, its steep, treacherous steps carved into the ice, a jagged scar across the mountainside, the deep-cut steps appearing impossibly steep from this height. It was a temporary, seasonal monument to the countless Stampeders who had climbed them with backs bent under impossible loads.

From up here, the scope of it, the sheer brutality of the climb was undeniable. Tiny black figures of men wound their way upwards, some still hauling their last loads on foot, refusing to pay the tramway's fares. Further below, at the incline's foot in a narrow basin was The Scales; and, beyond that: Sheep Camp. Both places were sprawled out in a patchwork of tents with acres of supply caches, wooden structures and the gathered Stampeders waiting their turn to climb. Despite their sprawl, mankind's presence was dwarfed by the imposing Coastal Mountains that dominated the skyline. Smoke from cooking fires twisted into the air, and groups of sled dogs and horses waited to unload at the tram stations. The powerhouse of one tramway belched out a continuous torrent of acrid black smoke.

Another set of tramway cables extended from Sheep Camp towards the tree line, marking the route on further west towards Canyon City, Dyea, and then: the coast.

The descent continued, and as he passed over The Scales he listened to the squeal of the cables, the whistle of the wind, and the distant, muffled noises of men and machinery working below. The tramway carried him lower, then gradually the angle lessened. The tension in the cables eased, the descent slowed, and the chaos of wind and motion began to ease.

The details of Sheep Camp became clearer, the crowded trails, the bark of sled dogs, the organized chaos of Stampeders sorting through their supplies and the various cargoes being loaded onto tram cars. The air smelled of wood smoke and wet fur, a sharp contrast to the icy emptiness of the Pass above.

Sheep Camp rose up to meet them, the end of the tramway finally in sight. The tram bucket jolted as it passed over the last pulley system, the momentum shifting as it prepared to stop.

With a final shudder, their cars glided into the station. Grant exhaled slowly, flexing his fingers where they had gone stiff from gripping the hanger bars. The descent had felt longer than it really was, the sheer drops had stretched every second into an eternity.

As the tram cars glided down into the station, workers moved forwards, pushing at the friction grips with steel bars, detaching the cars from the drive cable one by one.

Chalmers remained frozen in place. Once his bucket had been pulled aside, one of the tram workers, leant down and said in a light voice, “You can let go now.”

As the attendants unloaded the baggage from the cargo cars onto the muddy platform, Grant climbed out of his bucket. Rolling his shoulders to shake off the tension, he turned just in time to see Chalmers step out himself, legs slightly unsteady, face pale beneath his hat.

“You alright?” Grant asked.

Chalmers exhaled sharply. “If you ever make me do that again, I will shoot you.”

Grant chuckled, “I’ll keep that in mind.”

The cargo was already being stacked nearby, the workers efficient despite the cold.

Chalmers exhaled loudly, “Thank God,” he muttered, more to himself than anyone else.

Grant smirked. “See? We didn’t die after all.”

Wood and Sergeant Pringle were already waiting for them near the edge of the platform. Wood, ever the stoic figure, watched the unloading with mild interest. Pringle, arms crossed over his chest, looked imposing. The exact deterrent they needed from any outside interest in their cargo.

“You two look like hell,” Wood remarked dryly. “I thought we might have to send a crew up to pry you off the cable.”

Chalmers grunted. “I’d rather face a firing squad.”

Pringle let out a low chuckle. “That could still be arranged.”

Chalmers muttered something unkind under his breath, brushing snow from his sleeves. The workers finished unloading their heavy baggage, and soon, everything was stacked in front of them the eight regulation dunnage bags and the two Gladstone bags. Pringle dropped the dunnage bag from the Chilkoot's duties on top of the others to complete their collection.

Wood, hands clasped behind his back, surveyed the load and gave a slight nod. "Everything accounted for, good."

"What's next? Grant asked. "How are we looking for transportation?" Eyeing the number of ill tended, wandering horses around the camp, he added, "Looks like we won't be paying much for transport."

Pringle snorted, nodding toward a cluster of ragged-looking mounts huddled near an old corral. "You could trade a cup of coffee for a horse here, or less. Most got turned loose when their owners realized they'd be useless to climb the pass. Half of 'em are starved and will drop dead in a mile."

"We found that musher that Belcher mentioned," Wood said.

"Draper? The honest one?" Grant asked.

"I don't know about honest," Pringle said, shaking his head. "That's a rare enough commodity around here."

Chalmers sighed, "At this point, I'd settle for 'not a swindler.'"

"We settled on reliable," Wood answered. "He's securing us some mounts and will bring them on by. Until then, we stand ready and on guard."

Grant exhaled, adjusting his gloves. The descent might be over, but their journey was far from finished. Now, on the American side of the border and amongst the chaotic jumble of this tent camp, he felt more exposed than when he was dangling from a bucket hundreds of feet in the air.

Within the hour, Draper had arrived, bringing with him six reasonable mounts. They certainly wouldn't have passed muster on the Canadian side of the border, but the Mounties were not in any position to waste time or haggle, they wanted to be on the move.

As Wood oversaw the loading of the horses, he checked each of their bags with meticulous care. Pringle stood nearby, scanning the restless crowd with a practiced eye. His rifle never strayed far from his hands.

While Grant adjusted the saddle straps on his horse, he asked Wood, "You trust him?" nodding toward Pringle.

Wood didn't answer immediately. He secured the last strap on one of the Gladstone bags before replying. "Trust doesn't come easy out here," he said finally. "But Belcher wouldn't send us a fool."

Pringle, overhearing them, gave a sly smile. "That's just about the nicest thing anyone's said about me all year."

Wood ignored the comment, shaking his head as a wry grin cracked across his usually stern face.

"Mount up Gentlemen, next stop: Dyea."

CHAPTER XI

A Temporary Refuge

Much like its more infamous sibling and nearby competitor Skagway, Dyea was a rough and hastily assembled place. It was the kind of town that could only exist on the edge of civilization. A frontier hamlet where the raw ambition of thousands of hopeful prospectors collided with the harsh realities of life in the wild. The boomtown air was undeniable, but so was an undercurrent of unease. Stampeders milled about the muddy streets, restless. Most were new arrivals, but there were some who had returned from the interior, having abandoned the struggle and were now looking to book their passage back south. The rugged snow-capped Coastal Mountains loomed in the distance as the wind off the inlet coursed over the mouth of the Taiya River. It carried a sharp, cold and salty bite.

The town's narrow, unpaved roads were muddy and rutted from the incessant flow of wagons, sleds, horses and boots that trudged through town. Many of the buildings were little more than shacks, their façades weathered by the relentless winds and salt air. The smell of wet timber mixed with the sharp scent of saltwater and the ground, perpetually damp underfoot, gave the whole town a soggy, miserable feel.

Compared to their intense crossing of the Chilkoot Trail, to the Mounties, the route to Dyea had felt almost welcoming. The established wagon trails between Sheep Camp and Dyea were easy to travel, if it hadn't been for Grant's horse. The rental could be described as a back wrong horse, wretched, shabby filly. A flighty, incapable nag that should have not been long for the glue factory. It fought Grant and his load of the cargo the entire way.

When it wasn't bucking it had been jumping at its own shadow. Grant wished they had been able to bring Sophie and their other horses over the Chilkoot rather than have Orr and Tukey return them to the detachment at Bennett, along with their fallen comrades. Aside from that one low-quality mount, their transit to the coast had passed smoothly and without significant incident. All the traffic filing past them in earnest towards Sheep Camp were myopic to anything but their own journey to reach the Klondike. The harsh conditions and events of the last days had left their mark on each Mountie. For now, they hoped to catch their breath, regroup, and prepare for the important next steps in their journey.

Inspector Wood stood on the porch of the Cheadle Hotel, a two-story structure that despite its recent construction was already appearing as worn as the town itself. The hotel had served as a refuge for many new arrivals passing through the area on their way north. It was as close to the wharves as the Mounties could manage. It offered little more than a bed and basic sustenance in exchange for the exorbitant prices that were the norm in the Alaskan boomtowns. The hotel's interior was no better, with a musty, stagnant air that clung to the wood panelling. Even in the dim light of the main floor's common room, the dust never seemed to settle.

Inside, the Mounties had claimed a set of rooms in one corner of the hotel for themselves. The air was thick with tension. Despite this opportunity to relax, none of them were able to unwind their own internal mechanisms after their harrowing journey over the Chilkoot. In fact, the down time seemed to have had the opposite effect. They had arrived, four days earlier, but already it felt like they had been stuck in the place for months. The days bled together as they took turns guarding the precious cargo they had brought from Bennett. In a constant state of vigilance, they stayed inside as much as possible. They ate in shifts and took turns sleeping. The nights were restless as they kept their watch. Each creak of the hotel's wooden beams, each distant voice calling out from the muddy streets put them on edge. The longer they stayed in Dyea, the more they worried someone might come to snatch their cargo right out from under their noses. They had left two men dead on the Chilkoot, and though they had pressed on, the loss weighed heavily on each man. Wood knew that Grant felt that burden sharply as Milton's outlaws had been gunning for him specifically. As he surveyed the town from the porch, he couldn't shake the feeling that more men would be coming.

Wood adjusted the brim of his hat to shield his eyes from the blinding sun that had burnt its way through the overcast sky. The Mounties had been waiting, watching, and hoping the storm of trouble that seemed to follow them would pass on by. He could feel the tension of waiting creeping under his skin, like the cold that gnawed at him even though the temperature was mild. He had opted for Dyea over Skagway, reasoning that the relative calm and distance from Soapy Smith's hunting grounds might afford them a few days of undisturbed rest and planning. Though not without its own risks, it was a place to lay low, at least for the moment, until they had news of the ship that would carry him out of the territory south to Victoria. With the precious cargo of gold and money secured in their rooms and under continual guard, their next moves had to be measured, with every decision carefully weighed.

The sound of boots on gravel reached his ears, and Constable Grant, the chaos of the past days taut across his face, climbed the porch's steps to join Wood.

"This place, it smells of desperation," Grant muttered, wiping his brow with the sleeve of his jacket despite the cool spring air.

Wood nodded in agreement. "Desperation and greed. They all seem to think the Klondike is the answer to all their problems." His eyes wandered over the town. The streets were filled with all manner of people: prospectors, traders, and a handful of adventurers who had no clear purpose but to chase their fevered dreams of gold. The air was filled with the chatter of foreign tongues: German, Scandinavian, Russian all mingling with the familiar accents of Canadians and Americans.

The tide was out, exposing the muddy flats of the estuary and the skeletal remains of old boats that had been abandoned by the earlier waves of prospectors. The smell of rotting fish and seaweed mixed with the stench of the town, creating a pervasive odour that could not be avoided. Out at the far end of the port's long wharf, small boats were arriving and departing, the shouts of the dock workers filled the air as they shifted cargos from the end of the pier down to heaped staging areas at the town's edge.

"I can't shake the feeling that we're being watched," Grant said, his voice barely above a whisper. He leaned against the railing beside Wood, his eyes scanning the area. "We stand out too much."

Wood didn't respond immediately. Instead, he took in the scene, the small groups of men gathered around fire pits, their faces haggard from long days of hard labour and poor nutrition. Some smoked as they talked and a few kept to themselves, avoiding eye contact with the others. Every now and then, a man would glance up at the hotel, see the red serge jackets, their eyes lingering just a moment too long. Wood could feel the tension in the air. He had never been one to trust the locals in places like this. Too many of them had something to gain and nothing to lose. Grant's concern mirrored his own, but his duty as an officer of the North-West Mounted Police was clear. Their job was to maintain order and stay on mission, no matter the chaos surrounding them. And so far, despite the ambush and the loss of men, they had done just that.

"Best we don't mistake their inaction for indifference," Wood said after a pause. "They're waiting for something, or someone. We're not welcome here. You can see it in their eyes."

"Do you think Soapy's men have made it this far?" Grant muttered as he watched the long queues of men waiting outside the small post office. He wondered if the same sight would be waiting for him in Skagway, but that mission was yet to come so he banished the thought. There was still a set of very dangerous hurdles to be cleared before he could turn his attention to that challenge.

"We have to assume they have," Wood replied, his voice grim. "I would be surprised if he hadn't already gotten word of our arrival." He paused, then added, "Let's hope your little ruse has worked. Otherwise, if we linger here much longer, we'll become targets."

"Your ship's got to be docking in Skagway soon," Grant said, more in hope of hearing some news than anything else.

Wood could see the weariness in Grant's eyes. There had been no time to grieve the loss of their comrades, no time to process the danger they had been through. The Mountie's stoic professionalism had been tested to its limits on this mission. Wood had initially been suspect of the younger Constable, yet over the course of their journey the stakes had remained high, the threat from Smith's gang had only grown stronger and Grant had risen to the occasion. Their journey together had started under the weight of suspicion and tension, but that all had disintegrated after the attack at Deep Lake.

To Wood, the air in Dyea felt thick with the threat of impending conflict, and that danger was waiting for them just around the corner. Wood stood straighter, his posture rigid, as a faint noise echoed down the street as voices rose to become shouts. The two Mounties turned toward the sound, alert, but it was only a group of prospectors arguing over supplies.

Turning back towards their view towards the long wharf, they saw the news they had been waiting for. Striding off the long wharf came a tall man, his frame wearing the unmistakeable red serge uniform jacket and Biltmore Stetson.

"Hello, we've got something, Wood said, his expression hardening. "Let's hope he brings good fortune."

Wood pushed off from the railing, while Grant's gaze sharpened. He saw the crisp uniform, the man's deliberate steps. Soon, he could make out the four upward pointing chevrons on his sleeves of the red jacket. It was Staff Sergeant Hyles. He was a solid man, not one to rush into a situation but never one to delay when duty called. He had the air of someone who'd seen his fair share of trouble and had a proven ability to handle it.

"We won't be left in the dark for much longer," Grant remarked, his tone barely concealing the underlying tension.

As Hyles reached the hotel porch, he paused briefly, giving a curt nod to both men. "Inspector. Constable," he greeted them, his voice low and gravelly.

Wood, in his usual fashion, didn't waste time on pleasantries, "Staff Sergeant, what's the news?"

Hyles' gaze flicked to the hotel door before he stepped closer, lowering his voice, "The Tartar's arrived in Skagway."

"About time!" Grant exclaimed.

"I've got some bad news, though," he added bluntly. "I'm afraid it's not going to make your day any easier, Grant."

Grant tensed slightly, though his face remained impassive. "What is it?"

"There's a bounty on your head. Two thousand dollars. Dead. That kind of money will make plenty of desperate men take any kind of risk to collect."

Grant's gaze darkened. "Who's funding it?"

"Who do you think?" Hyles replied, his voice sharp. "The word's out and it won't take long for someone to act on it."

Grant's stomach tightened and his hand instinctively went to the holster at his waist. "This just keeps getting better and better."

"Soapy Smith, right?" Wood asked.

"If I were a betting man, that would be a safe and solid wager," Hyles replied.

Wood followed up, asking, "How do you know, Sergeant?"

"I got word through Grant's friend Jorge," Hyles explained. "He's been keeping an eye on things in Skagway. We've both been spreading your rumour around the saloons."

"Best we take the remainder of this conversation inside," Wood suggested.

Grant let out a quiet breath. "This is going to get ugly."

"Aye, you're not wrong there," Hyles replied.

As the three men stepped inside the hotel, the atmosphere around them seemed to electrify and in that moment, the town of seemed to pulse with a new and dangerous energy.

CHAPTER XII

A Blown Cover

The sun had barely begun to dip behind the peaks west of Dyea as Inspector Wood paced the worn floorboards of their hotel room. Hands clasped behind his back, his posture was stiff with a mixture of impatience and unease.

Outside, the bustle of the small town continued without interruption as merchants and prospectors continued their late-afternoon routines, carrying goods from the docks to the makeshift shops that lined the narrow streets. The Mounties could hear the shouts from the street, the rumble of traders wheeling barrels along the wharf, and the faint clink of metal and clatter of wheels on rough roads as wagons passed by the hotel.

Within the confines of their dimly lit rooms, a much darker atmosphere lingered, one of unease and impending danger that none of them could escape or dispel. The Mounties had hoped the low profile they had kept would not attract any attention, but their hopes were being dashed by the news Staff Sergeant Hyles had brought. They were not naive enough to believe they ever held the luxury of time, but they had hoped for a little more.

As Pringle stared out the window at the street below, Chalmers was laid out on one the beds, staring at the ceiling as he listened to Hyles lay out the scenario for them.

Grant, sat stiffly in a chair in the corner beside the stacked pile of their baggage. He looked between the two men. His mouth was a thin line. He had been silent for the past few minutes, but his nerves were starting to show, his fingers tapping restlessly on his knees, his jaw clenched. A bounty on his head wasn't exactly a surprise, not after the ambush on the Chilkoot, but hearing it confirmed made it even more real to him.

Hyles continued as he said, “Smith has eyes and ears everywhere. He has people watching the passes and they’ve been monitoring every ship coming in and out of Skagway. The question isn’t how he knows about anything, but how long does it take for word to reach him?”

Wood’s face hardened, “We have to presume he’s heard that we’re here.”

“That’s the best course,” Hyles agreed. “He certainly knows about you Inspector. Grant’s rumours have reached his ear.”

“Do you know if he believed it?” Wood asked.

“No, I don’t. When it comes to Smith, unless he makes it obvious, he’ll neither believe nor doubt anything on anyone’s say so. We can expect him to be at the docks to make up his own mind about you.” The Sergeant shifted uncomfortably, “And he’ll come in force.”

Wood let out a sharp exhale, running a hand through his short, cropped hair. He’d known this was possible, but hearing it confirmed made it more real, more immediate. Smith’s gang was no longer a distant or theoretical threat; they were here, and they were waiting for them.

“What about the price on Grant’s head? They’ve already tried to collect on it once. We lost two men because of Smith’s bounty.”

“Word’s spread. A bounty like that doesn’t stay quiet for long, especially in a town like Skagway. It won’t be long before Dyea hears about it too. For that amount of money, it’s not just Soapy’s men we’ll have to worry about; any man desperate enough will be looking to claim that prize.”

Grant’s mind was working over the options. His thoughts were racing, yet he had to remain calm. He had to think several moves ahead, just like a game of chess. But Smith’s gang was no ordinary opponent. They had the manpower, the resources, and the network to hear about every move the Mounties made.

Grant stood up abruptly, his chair scraping against the floor with a loud screech. His voice cut through the room, “Soapy knows we're here. He's heard the rumour about Wood, so we stick to the plan."

Wood exhaled slowly, "That's risky."

"We already know they'll shoot first. If we change tactics, they'll come at us with everything they've got. Let them think we don't know any better."

Chalmer, a sceptical look on his face, asked, "We do nothing and just play into their hands?"

"Exactly," Grant said, his voice firm. "We stay predictable, we act as they presume we'll act. Any change and the story breaks down. It's not their hand being played, it's ours."

"That's one helluva bluff," Hyles observed.

Wood nodded, but there was a hard edge to his voice. "That's the idea. We need them to think they're the ones in control."

Chalmers rubbed his temples, clearly not sold on the plan. "It sounds like a death sentence to me."

"I never said it was foolproof," Grant replied, his tone clipped.

Wood interjected, "It's a chance we'll have to take. If we don't hold our nerve, we'll be compromised. We stick to the plan, but we need to get out of here before we're boxed in."

Hyles sighed, "This is a dangerous game you're playing Inspector."

"It is," Wood admitted. "But I'm playing to win. If we let the fear of what Smith may or may not do dictate our moves, then he's in control. There's no other option or alternative. In a sense, the choice is easy. It's already been made for us."

The room fell silent as the weight of Wood's words settled over the group. Tensions had been rising steadily, but now there was a new urgency. They had no control over what Smith and his gang might do. The next few hours would determine their survival.

"We stay together as a group," Wood added carefully. "If we separate, we risk splitting our strength." Wood stared pointedly at Grant, "We'll need to keep the situation from getting out of control. Any thoughts of sacrificing yourself to distract Smith, that is not an option for me. Understood?"

Grant met Wood's gaze. "Yes sir, I'm with you."

Hyles, whose mind was already turning over their options, rubbed his chin thoughtfully. "The moment we leave this hotel, we'll be walking into a potential hornet's nest. People will be watching and waiting."

"Which means we'll have to be ready for whatever they throw at us" Wood said, looking each man in the eye. "We leave at first light. Hyles, can you arrange a boat to take us to the Tartar?"

"I'll get on it right away, Inspector," the Staff Sergeant replied.

"What if they come for us here?" Chalmers asked, his voice tight with unease.

"Then we fight," Grant said simply.

"Damn right," Sergeant Pringle growled. "Enough with the waiting. Bring them on."

The wind had picked up as the last light of the day faded behind the mountains. Twilight's departure cast a cold shadow over Dyea. In the distance, the faint sound of a ship's bell echoed across the water, a reminder that the clock was ticking and their window for escape was closing fast.

As the first rays of dawn broke, the town was still shrouded in the quiet of the early morning, yet to wake from its slumber. When the Mounties exited the hotel, shadows remained heavy across the narrow and rutted streets. The sun had yet to warm the mud, and its surface had hardened during the cool of the night. The men moved in efficient silence, their faces set with purpose. They held no illusions about what lay ahead, danger and uncertainty waited for them at every turn. However, they believed they held an advantage that would force the game to shift in their favour. The enemy may be waiting, but now they could only react to whatever the Mounties chose to do next.

As they filed out of the hotel, carrying their heavy baggage, Hyles was already outside, waiting for them. He had procured a pair of wooden hand carts, their sturdy frames swiftly loaded with the nine dunnage bags and the leather Gladstone bags along with their saddle bags and rolled Buffalo coats.

Wood watched the scene for a moment, his eyes scanning the street, taking in the stillness of Dyea's early morning. The quiet was eerie, if only amplified from their own anxieties. He gave a brief nod of recognition to Hyles.

"Lead the way, Chalmers," Wood said quietly, his voice steady but with an edge of urgency.

The Constable gave a brisk nod, then hefted his Winchester repeater and set off towards the wharves.

Pringle, one of the largest men among them, stepped forward and gripped the handles of one of the carts with a grunt. He was a hulking figure, his broad shoulders and thick arms a testament to years of hard work. Hyles followed suit, taking control of the other cart. Between them, the wheels groaned and squeaked with a steady rhythm as they protested under the weight of their loads.

Grant brought up the rear with Wood, both of their keen eyes sharp. Every building they passed, every shadow cast by the early light held the possibility of a threat. They had no idea where Smith's men might be. The threat of ambush hung over them like a dark cloud.

"Keep your eyes moving," Wood muttered under his breath.

Grant gave a sharp nod. "I'm ready," he muttered. His fingers flexed around the stock of his Winchester.

Chalmers' steps were long and sure, as he led them off the street and onto the long wharf. The air had a dampness to it now, with high tide, the saltwater of the bay filled their lungs as they moved over the waters of the estuary. The sound of their footsteps was muffled by the repetitive clunk-clunk-clunk of the hand carts crossing the wharf's wooden planks.

At the far end of the long wharf, a small tugboat waited, rocking gently with the rippling tide. The boat was small but sturdy, the vessel for their escape over the narrow waters of the inlet. It was their lifeline to Skagway, and they collectively hoped it would give them a chance to make it out of Dyea before Soapy Smith's men had a chance to catch wind of their movements.

Turning back towards the townsite, Wood's eyes scanned the wharf as the rest of the Mounties navigated its length. There were no signs of movement, no hidden figures in the shadows or men lounging about the docks as they might have expected.

"Almost there," Wood said, his voice carrying the weight of anticipation.

The faint hum of the tug's engine became clearer now, its low chugging sound overtaking through the morning's quiet.

Pringle and Chalmers pushed the carts forward with steady resolve and by the time they reached the boat, Chalmers was already at the edge of the wharf, gesturing for them to hurry. The small deck at the tugboat's stern was lined with ropes, coils of thick corded lines ready for use. Written in clear black paint across her stern read the name, "Clara".

As Wood reached the tug, Pringle and Hyles were already shifting the baggage off the carts. The saddle bags and rolled coats sailed through the air before Pringle grunted when he dragged the first heavy dunnage bag over to the boat, passing it to Chalmers who was already on board. Hyles followed suit, unloading with a surprising efficiency for such a large load.

Grant remained on the wharf, eyes scanning the area for any sign of movement. The wharf stretched long and empty behind them, the water gently lapping at the sides of the boats tied to the wharf. All remained quiet, yet the tension in the air seemed to increase with every passing second.

"Get aboard," Wood ordered Grant. "Tell the Captain to get underway."

Shortly after Grant boarded, the last of the bags were laid out on the tug's deck and Wood turned giving a quick signal. "Let's go," he urged.

Pringle and Hyles boarded, stepping cautiously over the narrow gangway as the tugboat's crew, two rough-looking men in worn coats and weathered hats cast off their lines. The tug creaked and groaned as it shifted in the water, the engine sputtering to life with a low growl.

Wood looked back toward the wharf once more, half-expecting to see figures emerging from the shadows in pursuit. But there was nothing. Only the stillness of the morning and the gentle swaying of the tide.

"Stay alert," Wood ordered, his voice firm.

As the tug slipped away from the wharf and Dyea began shrinking away behind them, Grant and Hyles exchanged a brief, knowing glance.

"To Skagway," Grant muttered under his breath.

As they pulled further away from shore, Pringle stood at the bow, scanning the horizon for any threats. The inlet's open water stretched out before them like an expanse of untamed possibility.

For now, they were safe, though they all knew it would never last. Smith's men were still out there, waiting for them to make a mistake. It was only a matter of time before they realized the Mounties were gone, and then: they would come after them.

For now, boarding the tug was a small victory. They had escaped the potential of being trapped in Dyea. The dangerous hours ahead would be faced with the same resolve that had carried them this far.

While the tugboat hummed steadily beneath their feet, Grant allowed himself to enjoy a rare moment of quiet.

CHAPTER XIII

Racing to Skagway

The chugging pulses of the tugboat's steam engine were steady, almost hypnotic. It cut through the cool morning air as the Mounties, their bags stowed tightly on deck, waited in tense silence. The narrow waters of the Taiya Inlet passed beneath them. A thin fog had settled over the water, thick enough to obscure the coastlines but light enough to allow their eyes to adjust as the boat veered southward on its short passage toward Skagway.

Wood stood at the stern constantly scanning the horizon. His face was set in hard lines, reflecting the weight of the moment. Their escape was neither complete nor a victory, not yet. They were about to gain a clear understanding of the many unknowns that waited for them at the Skagway docks. He turned to Grant, who had been standing silently beside him, his eyes also fixed on the fog ahead.

"Do you think they've realized we're gone?" Wood asked, his voice cutting through the hum of the engine.

Grant shrugged his shoulders, "We'll know soon enough. If Smith does have eyes everywhere, we might have a head start. A short one."

Wood nodded, and replied, "That may be all we need."

Grant could see the Inspector's mind turning. His own gut churned with uncertainty, and every instinct screamed at him through the sleep deprivation to stay vigilant.

Up at the tug's bow, Pringle and Chalmers were peering out ahead as the small vessel cut through the water. Hyles stood close by, his broad frame tense, his hand resting on the top of his revolver's holster. He too was scanning the water, waiting for any signs of trouble.

Suddenly, Hyles stiffened, his sharp eyes narrowing as he peered out across the inlet. Grant caught the shift in his posture and turned his attention toward the water. Just beyond the fog, a shadow moved. It was small but too deliberate to be anything but another boat. His heart skipped a beat as his mind raced through possibilities. It could be a local fisherman, another tug; or maybe someone just lost in the fog? Something told him it couldn't be anything else but a threat.

"Ahead, two o'clock," Grant murmured urgently to Wood.

"Chalmers, Pringle," Wood hissed, "Stand ready. We may have company."

The men tensed, instinctively reaching for their weapons. Chalmers and Pringle brought their rifles to their shoulders, muzzles down, with their gazes fixed on the approaching boat. Hyles stepped forward, pulling his Adams revolver from its holster, his eyes hard with focus. He was ready for whatever came their way through the fog.

The boat drew closer, its silhouette cleared the fogbanks to reveal itself in the grey morning light. It was another steam tug, though much smaller than the Mounties'. Its engine coughed and sputtered as it made its way towards them. As it neared the Clara, the figures on board became more distinct, four men, all armed with rifles and shotguns. Their faces were hard, weather-beaten, and their eyes locked onto the Mounties with a quiet intensity.

Grant's hand tightened on the around the stock of his rifle as the boat drew closer. No one else would be out here, this early, in this kind of fog, armed, without a purpose. These were Soapy Smith's men, there could be no doubt about it.

The smaller tug matched their speed and turned in a wide arc to run parallel with the Clara's course. They stood off and ran alongside them at what one would define as 'pistol shot'. Grant squared his shoulders, his gaze unwavering. He would not show fear, not now. Not to these men.

One of the men on the smaller tug called out, his voice carrying over the water. "Tugboat Clara. Heave to and prepare to be boarded."

His voice even and commanding, Wood said, "Sergeant Hyles, you tell the Captain not to stop under any circumstances. Clear?"

"Clear as crystal, Inspector," Hyles replied and stepped into the Clara's bridge to pass along Wood's instruction.

In a strong voice, Wood's projected reply spoke to his years of battlefield service, "Under whose authority?"

There was a pause, before the answer came back, "Skagway Port Authority."

"I think not," Wood replied.

"Are you refusing our direct order?"

"Stay where you are," Wood called back firmly, his voice cold and authoritative. The men were too close. Too bold. He couldn't allow them to board the tugboat. Not yet. Not without a fight. "We're not here for trouble, but we won't hesitate to defend ourselves."

As if on cue, Grant, Pringle and Chalmers all raised their rifles in unison and took steady aim at the men on the nearby tug.

"Mounties," the thug sneered, "Soapy's got business with you. He don't take kindly to being ignored."

"Soapy who?" Wood replied.

"Don't play dumb with us Copper," The man who spoke grinned a toothy, dangerous grin. "You know exactly who we mean. Which one of you is Grant?"

Grant shifted, stepping away from Wood, his rifle still aimed at the men across the water. "You're wasting your time," Grant said coolly. "You want a fight? You'll get one, but it's not going to be as easy as you think."

Smith's henchman considered Grant but did not reply. For a moment, there was a tense silence, broken only by the spluttering of the steam engines and the lapping of water against the sides of both tugs. The fog seemed to thicken around them, closing in like a shroud. The henchman turned his attention off Grant and back to Wood.

"What's it going to be?" asked the henchman. His voice dripped with menace, hoping to provoke them. "You're just going to keep running, like cowards?"

Wood took a steadying breath. He couldn't afford to let these men think they held any advantage.

"We're not running," Wood replied evenly, "and we're not looking for a fight either. Go tell your boss we're heading to Skagway. If he's got business with me, he can find me there."

The henchman's lips curled into a thin line. For a long moment, there was no response. Then, with a quick glance at his companions, he said, "Soapy already knows you're coming, Mountie. Don't think you're gonna waltz in there unchallenged. You're not as safe as you think."

With that, the henchman made a sharp motion with his hand, and the smaller tug began to pull away, its engine sputtering with effort. The other men looked back at the Mounties, their expressions filled with thinly veiled menace, before they disappeared into the fogbank.

Wood watched them leave, his gaze never wavering. But the moment they were out of range, he exhaled deeply, his shoulders sagging slightly with the relief of having avoided the confrontation.

"Not much of a conversation," Grant remarked dryly, his eyes still fixed on the fogbank.

"No," Wood agreed, "but they've sent their message loud and clear. They were waiting for us, and they're not going to let us slip into Skagway unnoticed."

Having returned from the bridge, Hyles holstered his revolver, but his face remained tense, his eyes scanning the fog for any further signs of trouble. "Smith won't be waiting alone."

Wood nodded sharply. "Of course he won't. After all this time, I'm almost looking forward to meeting the man."

As the Clara chugged forward, the Mounties fell into a grim silence. The threat of Smith's men was now a tangible thing, malingering like the pervasive fog around them. They were so close to Skagway, so close to the end of this long, dangerous journey. Soapy Smith had shown his hand. The Mounties had no choice but to keep moving forward, faster, harder, and with every ounce of their resolve. And so, they pressed forwards, leaving only the bubbling trail of their wake behind them.

CHAPTER XIV

Confrontation at the Docks

The Clara ploughed its heavy way through the water, its engine humming with a steady motion. Passing through a final curtain of mist, they rounded a bend in the coastline and Skagway came into view. The shoreline became clearer, the three long docks of the deepwater port stretched out before the town, and they could see figures moving along the long, narrow stretches of the wharves. It was bustling with activity despite the early hour. The mountain peaks beyond the town were sharp and jagged, their snow-capped tops just visible against the sky. The sound of the water against the hull of the tugboat seemed louder now, more pronounced. Grant's heart gave a slight jolt, he had been expecting this moment, but now that it dropped upon him like a heavy, wet coat.

Moored alongside one of the expansive wharves was the long white hull and the single engine stack of the passenger steamer S.S. Tartar.

"We're close," Grant said, breaking the silence. His voice was tinged with a mix of relief and caution. "There she is."

Beside him at the bow, Wood nodded but remained silent, his thoughts still circling around the danger that lingered like a shadow, following them even here. They would have to make their arrival swift, their movements measured. Knowing full well that Smith's men would not give up easily, Skagway was no sanctuary.

As they eased into the harbour, the tugboat's engine sputtered into silence. The tug's two crewmembers moved forward to the bow and let go the Clara's anchor with a sharp clang that echoed across the still harbour.

Hyles exited the bridge; his face was concerned. “Inspector, we have an issue.”

“What’s the matter?” Wood asked.

“Our Captain is spooked. He’s refusing to put alongside the Tartar, or the wharf. He wants us off now. It’s the spectre of Soapy Smith. He says we can use the Clara’s tender to row in.”

“Afraid to get shot in the crossfire is he?”

“Something like that,” Hyles replied.

“Can’t say I entirely blame him,” Wood said with a snort.

Wood’s fingers flexed around the railing. His eyes flicked toward the Tartar’s moorings, which ominously lay at the far end of the harbor. Between them and the ship, they could see the telltale signs of Soapy Smith’s influence: a cluster of heavily armed men waited on the wharf, ready for a fight.

“The word’s out,” Grant observed. “Smith’s men are everywhere.”

Hyles frowned and observed regretfully, “They’ll wait as long as they have to.”

Wood nodded but didn’t respond immediately. He took a deep breath, his thoughts momentarily spinning. Their escape had been a fleeting hope that had been dashed by the very men they had hoped to evade. There was no retreat, not now.

“The Tartar’s Captain knows we’re coming. I warned him before I came to Dyea yesterday.” Hyles added. “He has armed Navy Reservists on board.”

“They’re a long way off from here,” Grant offered.

“The only way out, is through. Get the small boat ready,” Wood ordered. “We’ll row in.”

Hyles nodded and walked away without another word, his heavy boots thudding against the deck as he went. Wood turned back towards Grant, his face serious.

“We need to be ready for this confrontation,” Wood said. “We’re not here to fight. We must get the bags onto that ship. All of them. That’s our priority. We make it to the wharf, and we hold the line, no matter what they try.”

Grant’s lips curled into a tight, grim smile. “We’ll get it done.”

The Mounties moved into action, gathering their baggage stuffed with the money they had so carefully guarded for nearly a fortnight. Each bag was an anchor, not just of wealth, but of the responsibility that weighed heavily on their shoulders.

As Hyles and Pringle readied the tug's small tender, the wind picked up, carrying with it the sharp scent of saltwater and the distant clang of a bell from the nearby wharf. Wood's sharp eyes scanned the docks again, searching for any sign of movement on board the ship, or from Smith's men.

"Stay sharp," Wood said as they moved toward the stern. "Once we make the wharf, unload and stand ready. We hold the gangway and don't let them surround us."

Grant and Chalmers nodded, each man gripping his rifle as though it were an extension of himself.

"Ready?" Grant asked quietly, his voice a steady thread of calm amidst the heavy silence.

Wood's lips pressed together in a thin line as he nodded, eyes never leaving the horizon. "As ready as we'll ever be."

He turned briefly to survey the crew of the tugboat, Captain and deckhands and noted their uneasy expressions. They knew exactly what the Mounties were walking into. It had taken little more than the arrival of *The Tartar* in Skagway to stir the pot of Soapy Smith's gang, and their presence at the docks made it clear they weren't leaving without a confrontation.

"Captain, we'll be getting off here," Wood said, his voice carrying across the deck. The captain, a stocky man with a thick beard and grizzled face, nodded and gave him a stiff salute.

"We'll stay put until you're clear," the Captain said, glancing nervously toward the wharf where Soapy's men were assembling. "Good luck, gentlemen."

Wood didn't acknowledge the Captain's words; his focus was already shifting to the task ahead. He and the others clambered into the rowboat swiftly. Hyles gave the signal, and with a grunt, Pringle and Chalmers took their places at the oars. The boat slid through the water with surprising ease.

From the wharf, it was clear that Smith's men were watching, their eyes tracking the tender's progress from the Clara. The Mounties reached the wharf after what felt like an eternity, the low slap of the waves against docks growing louder as they neared. The small boat scraped softly against the dock as Pringle and

Chalmers pulled in the oars, and Wood stepped onto the wharf first, a Gladstone bag in his left hand. Grant followed closely behind, his rifle at the ready, his eyes scanning the crowd gathering on the wharf above them, only the gangway down to the small dock lay between them and the thugs.

A dozen of Smith's men were already there, all looking rough and ready for trouble. At the front of the group was a man who could only be Soapy Smith himself. He stood tall, his dark eyes sharp, his face sporting a freshly shaped Mephisto beard. He wore a well-tailored blue suit, a gold watch chain across his waistcoat and a wide-brimmed hat that seemed to obscure most of his features. His pristine appearance was a commanding presence. The others flanked him were all heavily armed, poorly attired and wearing expressions that promised little more than violence.

Another bearded man stood beside Smith, wearing a rakish Boss of the Plains Stetson, and was speaking with the henchman who had confronted the Mounties earlier out on the inlet. After the henchman pointed out Grant, the man then leant towards Smith and spoke into his ear. Grant could see the flash of a threatening toothy smile cross Smith's face.

Grant's eyes locked onto Smith's. The air between them seemed to vibrate with the tension of a hundred unsaid words, and the weight of a thousand threats.

"Well, well," Smith called out, his voice smooth but carrying a dangerous edge, "The Mounties finally decided to show their faces in my town. Did you enjoy your little boat tour?"

Wood's expression was unreadable, though his eyes were calculating the scenario. "Chalmers, you and Sergeant Hyles get those bags off the boat. Pringle, Grant, follow me and then hold the gangway. Not one of them comes down to this dock."

"Well? Nothing to say?" Smith taunted them again.

Wood turned to face Smith and walked towards the gangway, with the rifle toting Grant and Pringle on his heels. As he began to climb the gangway, he replied, "I'm here on official business, Smith. I'll be boarding the Tartar and leaving. That's all."

Smith's lips twitched into a sardonic smile. "Is that right? I've heard differently. Word's been spreading about your little trip across the Chilkoot."

"Is that so?" Wood replied as he reached the top of the gangway. He stopped, set down the Gladstone bag and clasped his hands behind his back, blocking the way down. "How kind of you to notice."

At the foot of the gangway, an anxious Pringle and Grant waited and listened.

"Quite the security detail you've got there, Wood. Quite a lot of baggage too."

"Well, you know, us officers do like our creature comforts."

"Creature comforts I can understand. Did you get your hand caught in the cookie jar, Inspector?" Smith's eyes glittered with malice as he spoke.

"I wouldn't know anything about that, it's all just a misunderstanding that'll be sorted out in due course when I'm back in Ottawa."

"Interesting rumours I've heard. Dangerous rumours. Bribes, was it?" Smith asked, looking Wood up and down, clearly appraising the Mountie, sniffing out whether he was indeed the crooked man that the rumours claimed. "No, it just doesn't smell right to me. It seems to me, you've got something else on the go."

"Oh?" Wood shot back, "Do tell?"

"Those bags down there have anything interesting in them?"

Wood's jaw tightened. "I'm not here to entertain you, Smith. My personal effects are my own affair. Now, you can either let us pass, or we can settle this right here: you and I."

For a moment, there was silence. The two men stood facing each other, the Mounties on one side, the gang on the other. The crowd of onlookers had begun to grow, men and women were whispering, their eyes wide, eager for the outcome of this inevitable confrontation to appear. The tension in the air was thick, as though the entire town was holding its breath.

Smith's smile never faltered. He glanced over at his men, and then back to Wood. "You've got sand, I'll give you that. I think you forget that you're in Skagway now. This is my town, I wear the crown, and you're not going anywhere without my say-so."

Wood stepped forward, his gaze never leaving Smith's. "I'm not asking for your permission, Smith. My men and I will be leaving, and you're not stopping us."

The threat was implicit, but Smith seemed unbothered. He took a slow, deliberate step forward, his hand resting on the handle of a pearl handled revolver stuffed into his waistband. The two men stood nose to nose, neither one prepared to back down.

"Your men?" Smith observed and smiled. "So, they ain't your escort after all? The game's up. You really think it's that easy to fool me, Mountie?"

Smith's men shifted, some shuffling forward in anticipation, their hands resting on their weapons. The noose was tightening. For a moment, everything seemed to hang in the balance, until Smith raised a hand, signalling his men to hold back. His gaze locked onto Wood's once more, his smirk never fading.

"That man down there, Grant. What if I said you could leave if you give him to me?"

"I'd say take a long walk off this wharf."

"Now you've gone and hurt my feelings," Smith mocked him.

"I'm sure you've been told worse," Wood replied. "Will you let us pass or are we going to have a problem?"

"We're going to have a problem. A couple problems I think."

On the dock below, Hyles and Chalmers had joined Grant and Pringle at the foot of the gangway.

"Get out of my way, Smith," Wood said quietly, his eyes never leaving the criminal's face.

Smith took a long breath, his eyes flicking from Wood to the rest of the Mounties and the piled baggage on the narrow stretch of dock behind them. There was a flicker of calculation in his eyes, and Wood could sense the shift, the moment when Smith realized he had the upper hand.

"You can have your fight if you want it, Mountie," Smith said, his voice colder now, his smile disappearing. "TJ, tell the boys to make ready."

Texas Jack Vermillion, Soapy's second in command snapped his fingers and the cluster of men began to spread out across the wharf, weapons ready as they looked down on the Mounties.

Grant, Chalmers and Pringle rifles held their unwavering aim, poised to fire. Sergent Hyles drew his revolver from its holster, coked the hammer of its action and held it at the ready by his side.

Wood scanned the wharf as the gang spread itself out in its show of force and looked towards the Tartar. There was an imperceptible glint that appeared in his eye as he turned back towards the bearded smirk of Soapy Smith. He said, “How far are you willing to push this, Smith?”

The waiting crowd of onlookers, the Mounties and Smith’s gang all drew in an expectant breath. The situation had escalated too far and now threatened to spill over into an unavoidable display of violence and firepower.

The tense silence that had descended was shattered in an instant, not by gunshots, but by the long, sustained blast of the S.S. Tartar’s horn.

CHAPTER XV

God Bless the Royal Navy

Captain Pybus stood in the wheelhouse of the S.S. *Tartar*, his boots planted firmly on the wooden deck and swept one hand back through his greying hair. Moored alongside one of the long piers of Skagway's port, his current focus was a clerical one. Spread out across the room's main chart table, obscuring the detailed navigational charts of the Alaskan coastline, he sifted through a pile of the perpetual, yet pedantic logistical records from the last voyage.

As he reviewed the current state of the ship's stores, manifests and crew reports, Pybus listened to the ship's small expressions: the creak of wood, the soft rumble of the boilers belowdecks, the muted conversations of the crew at work on the deck outside. Bobbing gently on the cool waters, the Tartar's crew were far from idle as they prepared for the next wave of passengers set to board for their one o'clock departure.

Pybus had always preferred the solitude of the wheelhouse, the hum of the ship's movements and the constant rhythm of the sea lapping against the ship's hull than the grating frustration of passengers. *Human cargo is always the most challenging*, he mused to himself as he pored over the accumulated paperwork before him.

People equated to problems. They had only made port the day before, the passengers had not even begun to disembark when a Sergeant of the North-West Mounted Police came aboard, requesting an urgent audience with him. Now he was saddled with the responsibility of ensuring the safety of these Mounties, their cargo; and the other passengers coming aboard for the sailing to Victoria. Pybus much preferred the challenge and threat of dead reckoning navigation off a lee shore in a gale than the demands of managing people and their needs. Pybus had learned to trust his instincts over his long career at sea. Something was coming, and he had a hunch it wasn't going to be good. He forced himself to end his musings and returned his focus to the waiting paperwork around him.

His second-in-command, Lieutenant David Jenson, entered the cabin swiftly, his boots tapping on the floorboards as he made his way toward the chart table. Jenson's face was tight with concern as he came to a stop, saluting briefly before speaking.

"Captain, you wanted to be told when the Mounties arrived." Jenson said, his voice a mixture of concern and authority.

Pybus' brow furrowed, "Earlier than expected."

"They appear to be in a spot of bother."

Jenson was the type of man who didn't waste time, and the seriousness in his tone spoke volumes. Pybus glanced up, "What sort of bother?" he asked, his voice betraying a sharpness that matched the tension he had felt growing in the pit of his stomach.

Jenson handed him a spyglass. "Best you come aft, sir. There's a confrontation on the wharf. They seem to have encountered a group of armed men."

Without hesitation, Pybus took the spyglass from Jenson's hand and said, "Show me."

With determined, yet unhurried strides, Pybus and Jenson exited the wheelhouse and headed aft. Reaching the stern of the steamer's main deck, Jenson directed his attention towards the far wharf and its docks. Pybus extended the brass tubing of his spyglass with a snap and raised it. Peering through the eyepiece, he focused on the scene unfolding across the port. The Mounties were there, their red uniform jackets a stark contrast against the weathered wood of the lower dock. They were grouped together, in a tight formation, rifles at the ready at the end of a gangway. Pybus followed their steady aim up towards the wharf above. He could see their officer, ascending the gangway towards a large group of armed men. The gang were radiating the sort of arrogance Pybus had grown used to seeing in dockside criminals who thought they were untouchable.

Pybus' mouth tightened into a line as he observed the standoff. It seemed that the Mounties weren't backing down, but they were obviously outnumbered and out gunned.

"That's trouble," Pybus muttered under his breath, his grip tightening on the spyglass. He pulled it down after a moment, his gaze fixed on the wharf as he considered his options. "Mobilize the Reservists," Pybus ordered, his voice decisive. "Have them fall in at the double and go get the Mounties."

"Aye, Captain, I had them waiting," Jenson replied, and turned to call out to a blue jacketed man standing at attention nearby. "Warrant, take your sailors and quick march to the wharf. Go and collect those Mounties."

The Warrant Officer barked in reply, "Yes sir!"

As the Warrant Officer turned on their heel and disappeared inside the ship, Pybus issued further instructions, "Gather any idlers in the crew and break out the rifles, Jenson. If there's going to be a fight, I want every able man on deck, armed and ready to defend this ship."

"Aye," Jenson replied and already at a brisk walk, he left the stern to carry out his orders.

"And sound the ship's horn, long blast!" Pybus called out over his shoulder.

The Captain remained at the stern's hurricane rail, watching through his glass as the scene on the wharf continued to escalate. He could make out the frustration on the face of the Officer as they spoke to who could only be the gang's leader. The bearded man stood out with his expensive suit, a deep, dark blue that nearly matched the colour of the ocean, that was perfectly tailored, and polished boots that gleamed. *Could this be the infamous Soapy Smith?* Pybus wondered as he watched the bearded man waggle his finger at the Officer. If neither side backed down, there would be a fight. It would be short, sharp and bloody. He did not favour the Mounties' chances.

Belowdecks, the assembled Royal Navy Reservists, hand-picked for their ability to keep calm in the face of danger, were a mix of weathered sailors and fresh-faced eager recruits. Each man, their rifle at the ready, were exiting the ship, following their Warrant Officer. As Jenson marshalled the ship's regular crew he directed them to the weapons locker, where the ship held a small number of bolt action rifles. As they were being handed out, along with a box of cartridges to each crew member, Jenson barked swift orders.

"Two of you will guard the main gangway. No man comes on board without my permission. The rest of you, stand by the Captain at the stern and prepare to defend the ship."

The crewmembers, nodded in unison. Despite the sudden dangerous excitement, their faces were steely with resolve. Their rifle barrels shone in the low morning light as they moved with purpose to the stern. Captain Pybus, standing tall and resolute, nodded to the men who arrived behind him, rifles at the ready. The scene on the docks was growing more intense by the second. He knew that every passing moment could bring about the tipping point: an explosion of violence that would leave no room for negotiation.

"No man fires without my express order," he barked.

As the crew took up their positions, Jenson was making his way back to the wheelhouse. Climbing the exterior steps, he could see the blue-jacketed Royal Navy Reservists, in formation, at quick march down the wharf swiftly closing the distance between them and the armed mob. There was no panic in their steps, just quiet professionalism. They were men who had weathered storms, fought battles, defended ships and now prepared for a fight on land.

Back on the wharf, the tension between the Mounties and Soapy Smith's gang had reached its boiling point. Smith's bluster and bravado was backed by the armed men arrayed around him.

At the top of the gangway, Inspector Wood stood resolute against the tide of criminality that threatened to rush him and his men for the prize of the customs duties piled on the dock below.

Wood held Soapy Smith's stare and asked him, "How far are you willing to push this, Smith?"

The gangster seemed to catch the light that had flashed in Wood's eye and was about to reply when the long, sustained blast for the Tartar's horn split the air.

When Smith turned to look towards the ship, his eye widened as he saw the formation of Royal Navy Reservists only a stone's throw away, approaching with disciplined efficiency along the wharf. Their boots thudded heavily against the wooden planks, their rifles held tightly at the ready, their faces grim and resolute. For a moment, Smith hesitated. His eyes darted from the armed men marching toward him towards Wood and the other Mounties. He could feel the shift in the atmosphere, the balance of power had slipped out of his control.

"If you want your fight," Wood's firm voice added. "It won't just be with me."

"Company, halt!" The Warrant Officer barked.

The Reservist's formation halted, their boots crashing to the planks of the wharf in unison.

"Company. Present arms!"

The formation raised their rifles on cue and aimed down the wharf at Soapy's gang and the assembled onlookers beyond them. Cries of surprise and terror punctuated the air as the crowd began to back away from the confrontation's new line of fire in panic.

Wood, hands still clasped behind his back, did not let the relief show on his face, but inside, the pressure that had been building in his chest seemed to lessen. The arrival of the Royal Navy and the full weight of British authority had brought a semblance of order to this chaos.

At the same time, the presence of the navy men on the wharf made the confrontation even more dangerous. Soapy Smith's gang was no longer just facing a handful of Mounties; they were now standing against an armed military force, a group that was as capable in combat as they were in their duties at sea.

The wharf now felt like a powder keg, each moment adding more tension to the already volatile situation. The men of Smith's gang, still forming a ring around Wood and the gangway down to the money shifted uneasily, their fingers twitching toward their weapons.

Wood's eyes remained fixed on Soapy Smith as the moment stretched out, each second feeling like an eternity.

Then, Smith stepped back, but only slightly, his hands rising in mock surrender. His smooth voice, dripped with mockery, "You've made a mistake, Inspector," Smith finally said, his voice cold but laced with the faintest hint of resignation. "I thought I might have a little fun with you, but this has gotten out of hand. Wouldn't you agree?"

Wood didn't respond at first. His gaze was steady, unyielding. He wasn't fooled by Smith's charm or his rhetoric. He knew that if the situation was going to be resolved without bloodshed, it would come down to nerves and who could outlast whom.

"I would," he agreed. "You are right though, this game is over. Now, if you'll excuse me. My men and I have work to do."

Smith's lips curled into a half-smile, though it didn't reach his eyes. He tilted his head slightly, as if considering Wood's words carefully. "Maybe you're right, Wood," he said, his voice softening just enough to make Wood pause. "Maybe I pushed too far."

Wood broke his gaze with Soapy and turned to look at his men on the dock below and called out, "Sergent Hyles, let's be about our business."

Down on the dock, Grant exhaled and muttered, "Bloody hell."

Chalmers agreed through gritted teeth, "Tell me about it. I damn near pissed myself."

Sergent Hyles holstered his revolver, and said, "Come on, let's be quick about this and get the hell out here."

Pringle, Grant and Chalmers each slung their rifles over their backs as they walked to their piled baggage.

"We're going to need help with this," Grant began to say, but Pringle shouldered him out of the way.

The Sergeant then swung two of the dunnage bags over his broad shoulders and then picked up another two and growled, "Just get moving."

Hyles, another big man, matched Pringle's feat and nodded towards the remaining dunnage bag, the last Gladstone bag and their assorted coat rolls and personal effects, telling Chalmers and Grant, "Hurry up."

Chalmers hefted the dunnage bag, a pair of their rolled coats along with a saddlebag and grunted at the effort. Grant grabbed the remaining Gladstone, his coat and saddlebags. While he climbed the gangway he took a moment to be amazed by the sheer physical feat of the two Sergeants.

Chalmers picked up on Grant's thoughts, observing, "Remind me never to get on their bad side."

As Chalmers and Grant arrived on the wharf, one rank of Reservists had parted the crowd and formed a protective perimeter on the other side of the gangway. On the other side of the Navy's rifles, Soapy Smith, Texas Jack and the rest of the gang stood by watching as the Mounties shifted their heavy baggage down the wharf towards the waiting Tartar. Grant's eyes flickered towards Soapy Smith as he passed by, keeping his back straight, rifle slung over his shoulder. His hands gripped his baggage with firm determination, a man on a mission.

"Would you look at that, a dead man walking," Texas Jack called out, provoking a sniggering laugh from the assembled henchmen.

Grant turned towards the taunt, his eyes burning. He dropped the bags with an audible thump and stared at Texas Jack.

"Oooooh," the criminal mocked. "Did I get your attention, Mr. Grant?"

Wood had remained by the gangway and stepped beside Grant. "Leave it alone," he quietly warned the Constable and pointed towards the Reservists.

Grant shifted his gaze to Soapy Smith, the man who had ordered his death. The gangster's dead eyes looked back without any sign of emotion or light. Like a snake with a cruel smile, the man couldn't leave things alone.

"You know," Smith called out, voice smooth with an unsettling confidence, "Someone put a nice little bounty on your head. Did you hear? People are talking about you. They want to meet the Mountie who can't be bought, the one too proud, self-righteous and stubborn for his own good. The side effects of that kind of behaviour, they can be fatal."

"You're wasting your time and money Soapy," Grant replied, his voice hard. "Your man Milton already tried to collect. He ended up dead. That fatal side effect's waiting for anyone else stupid enough to try."

"You sure about that?" Smith asked. "Milton wasn't all that capable. I hope no one else got, hurt."

Grant balled his fists, but before he could speak again, Wood's voice rang out, authoritative and unyielding. "That's enough, Smith."

Wood positioned himself between Grant and Soapy. His hand rested on his holster, though he made no move to draw his sidearm. His mere presence, calm and confident, sent a clear message, there would be no further escalation.

Soapy gave a small, mocking bow, a sardonic grin spreading across his face. "Of course, Inspector. I was just having a friendly chat with your man here. No harm in that, right?"

He chuckled darkly, looking around at his gang. He knew when the game was up. His men were already backing away, some muttering under their breath.

"I'll see you soon, Grant," Smith said, his voice low, almost a whisper but loud enough to be heard. "Very soon."

"Time to go, Constable" Wood said and turned to face Grant. "Take the Gladstone, I'll collect the rest of your effects."

Grant held Soapy's eyes for a moment longer, with a look that said far more than words ever could. He then stooped down to pick up the Gladstone bag. Without another word he turned away from the gangsters and walked towards the haven the Tartar offered them.

Wood collected the last of the baggage, then followed Grant without another word. As the Mounties left, Smith's predatory eyes never left their backs. He called out one final offering over the shoulders of the departing Reservists, "Why don't you stay in Skagway for a while, Inspector? You and your men are always welcome. Stop by the Parlor, have a drink on me."

And with that, Smith turned on his heel, signalling to his men to follow. As he left, he said, "How very disappointing, TJ. I thought Grant would have been taller. Let's go boys, Whiskey's a calling me."

Grant's pace never faltered as he climbed the gangway to step on board the Tartar. They had made it, achieving their goal. Their precious cargo was safe, and they had stood up to the face of criminality, if not the devil himself. But inside, a part of him couldn't help but wonder if Smith's words carried more weight than he was willing to admit. Skagway's underworld had been dealt a blow, but there would be other battles waiting for him.

The Mounties were in enemy territory, and the fight was far from over.

Captain Pybus approached Wood as he stepped off the Tartar's main gangway, and greeted him, "Inspector, welcome aboard."

Wood replied, "We're grateful for your help Captain, and god bless the Royal Navy."

CHAPTER XVI

Safe Passage

The S.S. *Tartar* rode tall in her moorings, its masts towering over the shoreline like a sentinel watching over the port of Skagway. Her single funnel was beginning to pump out steam, evidence that her boilers were being stoked and brought up to temperature, ready for her upcoming departure. Just approaching midday, the sun had peeked through the clouds to cast slow moving shadows across the port and flashed bright off the ship's fresh white paint.

The Mounties filtered down the ship's main gangway to the pier. Their mission had been accomplished, the gold, coin and banknotes of the Klondike's customs duties were safely secured in the Tartar's hold. The threat of Soapy Smith had temporarily been pushed aside. Wood and Chalmers would stay aboard the ship and make their passage to Victoria. Yet, a heaviness still hung in the air over them, unspoken and ever-present. The fleeting thrill of victory and relief they had felt had dissipated as quickly as the morning's mist. The realization that neither Thompson nor Young were there to enjoy the moment made any sense of success feel bittersweet.

Sergeant Hyles had already returned to detachment's office in town. For Grant, what came next was rapidly filling his thoughts. For him, the danger was far from over, and the bounty on his head loomed like a spectre over every moment to come.

Pringle stepped forward, his towering frame casting a shadow across Chalmers and Grant. "Well, gentlemen," he said, his voice as gruff as ever. "I'll be taking a tug back to Dyea. I've got a few things to settle up there before I return to the Chilkoot."

Wood turned to him, his face unreadable as he adjusted the strap of a large satchel across his shoulder. "Take care, Pringle. Thank you for your help. And keep an eye on the trail. It's never truly safe out there." He then offered his hand.

Pringle nodded, and shook Wood's hand, "Inspector."

His heavy boots rang out on the wooden boards as he turned to leave. "Don't get comfortable Grant. Skagway's never as quiet as it appears. I wouldn't trust a soul here beyond Sergeant Hyles."

With that, Pringle walked away, his steps brisk and speedy for such a large man. The remaining Mounties stood silently for a moment, watching the Sergent's back recede into the distance, each of them considering their next moves.

"I won't keep you two," Grant offered. "I should be getting to the detachment and catch up with Hyles."

Wood's eyes flicked towards Chalmers, who stood beside him, ever watchful. "Grant," Wood said, "We'll escort you there. I feel the need to stretch my legs. I won't take Soapy up on his offer of a drink, but we may as well see some of the town."

Grant, who had been silent since their cargo had been locked safely away, finally allowed himself a brief exhalation of relief. He had weathered the storm so far, but there was always more to come. He had been worrying about his first walk down the streets of a town that may want him dead.

"I appreciate it," he said, his voice a bit rougher than he expected. Hefting his saddlebags, rifle and Buffalo coat, they set off together.

With the sound of their boots echoing along the wharf, the trio began their journey down the long pier towards the townsite. The smell of saltwater mingled with the heavy scent of lumber and the acrid tang of coal smoke. The three piers themselves stretched out into the inlet, like slender fingers scratching out mankind's tenuous hold on the coast. Once at the shore, they intersected with warehouses and the makeshift shops that had sprung up to cater to the ever-growing population of hopeful miners, traders, and adventurers arriving in the town. The air was filled with the clang of metal, the thud of crates being dropped onto the wooden planks, and the occasional shout of a sailor or stevedore calling out to one another. Skagway's industrious stretch of waterfront served as the gateway between the outside world and the rugged wilderness of the Klondike. This primary deepwater port was the favoured entry point for those headed to the gold fields, and the docks were vital in sustaining the growing town's economy and its frantic pace.

For the Mounties, however, Skagway was a place where the rule of law was tenuous, where tension simmered just beneath the surface, and where every decision could have far-reaching consequences in the dangerous game of the gold rush. Hastily built, rough-hewn structures lined the edge of the waterfront. Some buildings were temporary, wooden shacks or canvas topped structures that housed everything from dry goods to shops to saloons. The further the Mounties walked into town the more permanent and larger the wooden warehouses became. Built to handle the volume of trade, old or new, these buildings were weathered and grimy from their constant exposure to the salt and sea air. The waterfront seemed to be ageing before their eyes.

Passing the ramshackle shops, the hurried footsteps of miners, traders and the new arrivals trying to make their fortune moved around the Mounties' more casual pace. Amongst the melting pot of humanity, Grant felt that with every step he took through the streets, eyes remain locked on him. Curious, cautious eyes that may only have been noting the men in uniform who were walking in their midst. The bounty on his head made him presume otherwise. He felt hunted and Chalmers seemed to pick up on Grant's worry.

"The price on your head," Chalmers remarked as they moved through the busy port. His voice was casual, but there was a hard edge beneath it. "You don't get that kind of attention for nothing. You obviously caused more than a ripple in Soapy's world. I'm surprised it's not higher."

"I cost him a lot of money, that's all," Grant replied.

"Dead? You'll cost him even more," Chalmers guffawed.

Wood had been watching Grant from the corner of his eye. "It's more than money. You cost him reputation. You stopped his plans, and he hates you for that. Now, you... we, have foiled his plans again. He's got egg on his face. That's not a great look for some master criminal. I don't believe money matters anymore once that happens. He'll be stung again from this morning."

"I can handle it," Grant replied, his voice steady, though there was a hardness in his eyes. "If Soapy thinks he can scare me, he's mistaken."

"You're scared," Wood countered. "Hell, I'm scared for you. There's no way to prepare for the feeling of being hunted."

"All for doing the job," Chalmers added.

"Exactly," agreed Wood.

Grant let out a long breath. "Soapy can send as many men as he wants. They'll all meet the same fate."

Wood glanced at Chalmers, who gave a noncommittal grunt. It was clear that neither of them fully believed Grant's words. He was capable, there was no doubt of that. Even with their training, even with the support of the entire North-West Mounted Police, there was something unsettling about having a man like Soapy Smith setting his sights on you. None of them were foolish enough to think Grant's troubles with the Skagway underworld were over.

By the time they reached the detachment office, the midday sun was warming their backs. The Tartar's horn sounded in the distance, giving passengers notice of its imminent departure. The detachment had rented a small, single storey building, that looked more like a weather-worn shack than a place of authority.

"Here we are," Wood said as he came to a halt in front of the office.

"Thank you for the escort," Grant said to Wood and Chalmers.

"It's been an adventure," Chalmer told Grant as they shook hands. "Watch your back."

"I will, safe travels Chalmers. Enjoy Victoria."

"Give us a moment," Wood said to Chalmers.

The Constable nodded and began to walk back towards the port.

Wood placed a hand on Grant's shoulder, a brief moment of camaraderie shared between them. It wasn't much, but for Grant, it was enough to know that he wasn't entirely alone in this.

"If you need anything, lean on Sergeant Hyles. If you think for a moment that it's become too dangerous to stay? Get out of town and back over the mountains as soon as you can. I will support whatever you choose and back it up with Steele. Don't risk more than you must."

Grant heard the undertones of concern in Wood's voice. "I know," he said softly. "But I'm not running from him, or anyone."

"I understand that, just be smart about it," Wood advised him. "Being stubborn for stubbornness' sake gets men dead, whether you're a criminal or a copper."

Grant gave a wry smile, "Watch out, you're starting sound like a Stampeder."

"It does rub off on us, doesn't it?" Wood laughed. "Now that you're in charge of territorial mail, I'll send you a letter when we get to Victoria."

"Right, I'm not sure how I'm going to tackle that beast."

"Just like anything else, by starting. Little by little." Wood said and extended his hand.

Grant shook it firmly and said, "Thank you, Inspector."

"No, thank you. I'm sure we'll see each other again," Woof then removed the satchel hanging off his shoulder. He offered the bag to Grant by its strap. "You're going to need this."

"What's this?" Grant asked, taking the heavy bag."

"Operating capital," Wood replied. "The wheels of industry require grease. There's enough money going to Victoria, they're not going to miss this token amount."

"Graft?" Grant asked.

"Small graft," Wood replied. "Apparently I'm known for it."

With that, Wood smiled, turned on his heel and strode off to catch up with Chalmers.

As the door to the detachment office creaked open, Grant stepped inside, the warmth of the small room enveloping him. The faint scent of wood, ink, and the lingering residue of burned-out lamps greeted him as he looked around. The office was cramped, cluttered with papers, files, and maps strewn across the rough-hewn wooden desks. The faint glow of an oil lamp cast dancing shadows along the walls. A portrait of the Queen, a gun rack with a handful of rifles standing ready, and an open doorway that led through to another room further inside the shack. The space was small, but it was functional, a place where decisions were made, and orders were given. It had the feel of a place that had seen little care but plenty of work.

Wood and Chalmers had walked him this far, but now, as Grant stood at the threshold of the office, it was clear that the next steps would be his to take alone. He called out, "Hello?"

Sergeant Hyles appeared through the open doorway at the rear of the office, and greeted the Constable, "Grant. Any trouble finding us?"

"No issues whatsoever."

"Any other troubles?" Hyles asked, the poorly veiled question about the bounty.

"None, let's not fixate on that, please, Staff Sergeant." Grant replied.

"Understood," Hyles replied and leaned forward, his voice steady. "You're not alone in this, Grant. You have the support of the men here, and I'll help however I can. We'll leave it at that. For now, let's get this mail moving."

Grant met Hyles's gaze, the sense of respect that had developed over the past few days between the two men was evident. "What do I need to know?"

"For starters, it's an absolute mess."

"One step at a time," Grant replied. "How much mail are we talking about?"

"It's the sort of thing you need to see in order to understand the true nature of the challenge." Hyles answered, then asked, "You up for a walk back to the port?"

CHAPTER XVII

Soapy's Wrath

Nestled near the heart of Skagway's bustling waterfront was a place of both quiet opulence and seedy underworld intrigue. The moment you entered Jeff Smith's Parlor, the heady scent of tobacco smoke hung in the air, thick and heavy like a fog. It mingled with the pungent odours of strong distilled spirits, whiskey, gin, and the occasional hint of rum.

It was a space where the dreamer rubbed elbows with the desperate. Where prospectors hoping to strike it rich sat side by side with gamblers, crooks, and even the occasional lawman. The bar stretched along one side of the Parlor. Behind it, a row of bottles lined the shelves. The bartender, a burly man with a weathered face, was quick and practised with his pouring hand and even faster to sweep the patron's payments up. His eyes, however, remained sharp, always alert to the comings and goings of the crowd. He knew what went on in the Parlor, and he had learned to turn a blind eye when necessary.

At the far end of the room, a battered stand up piano sat in a corner. The music had stopped and there was a distinct tension between the walls of the narrow building. It was no longer simmering beneath the surface but had reached a rolling boil as the sound of crashing, splintering wood and malevolent cursing could be heard through the thin wall that separated the Parlor's main space from its back rooms.

The soft hum of conversation had once filled the space, the usual clink of glasses on polished wood punctuated by the murmur of voices had all become as silent as the grave once the crashing and swearing out back had begun.

Small groups of men, likely prospectors or merchants, sat in silence at their tables listening to the tumult without any expression on their drawn and haggard faces. Their clothes showed the strain of the harsh Alaskan wilderness, they looked like men whose dreams were now half-forgotten, and they drowned their disappointments in whiskey.

Others moved quietly about the room, always scanning for any sign of trouble. Things in the Parlor could turn violent quickly, and Soapy Smith's hired hands, big, burly men with sharp eyes and dangerous smiles, kept the peace, though it was always on their terms. A few of the men leaned against the walls, scanning the room for potential threats, while others lounged at the bar, their heavy boots clicking softly against the floor as they shifted their weight and listened to the continued cursing and crashing behind the closed door leading to their boss' private office.

It wasn't the first time Soapy had gone on a rampage. His waiting men exchanged uncomfortable glances, unsure of whether to intervene. But no one dared approach the boss when he was this worked up.

"Damn fools!" Soapy 's voice trembled with fury on the other side of the partition. "Do they think they can just walk all over me? These Mounties... this is MY town!"

Another loud crash was heard followed by silence.

Standing at the bar, one of Smith's enforcers, a grizzled individual named Rourke, observed to the barkeep, "Sounds like he's tiring."

"Careful Rouke," the barkeep warned.

"What? I'm just saying..." he protested.

The low hum of conversations slowly began to return in the face of the prolonged silence from the back rooms. Just then, the Parlor's front door creaked open. Texas Jack, Soapy's second-in-command, entered, his spurred boots making their familiar thud and jangle against the wooden floor.

"Where is he?" Texas Jack asked the barkeep.

"Out back. Watch it, he's in a mood," answered the barkeep.

As Texas Jack made his way to the door at the rear of the Parlor, Rourke called out to him, "Hey TJ, what's the story on that bounty? Is it still good?"

"Yeah Rourke, it's still good." Texas Jack replied. "Why don't you quit barking and hurry off like a good little doggie and go collect on it?"

"No need to be sore with me, TJ." Rourke replied.

"I ain't sore with you, I got other things on my mind."

"You got a mean way of being pleasant," Rourke countered.

Texas Jack stopped at the door, his hand on the knob, he turned and with a finality in his voice, said, "You gonna go do something for once, or not?"

"I'm going, I'm going. That Mountie's a dead man. I'm just gonna have me one more drink."

"Yeah, you do that," Texas Jack replied, turned the doorknob and stepped through to the Parlor's back rooms.

As he closed the door behind him with a low creak and click as the latch engaged, Texas Jack considered the scene before him. The wreckage of furniture, glassware, bottles and crates were strewn about the room. There was a murderous fire in Soapy's eyes, the veins in his neck pulsed, and his teeth were clenched so tightly that they could have cracked.

Texas Jack had seen this before, but it never made it any easier to watch. The showdown at the docks had been a humiliation, and the burning sense of failure would be searing a hole through Soapy's gut. He had been so sure that the Mounties would be easy, predictable pickings. Grant had thwarted him again. And now, here he was, stewing and alone in the wreckage of his own temper, the walls of the Parlor echoing with the chaos of his frustration. Texas Jack knew it wasn't wise to get in the way, but he was also a man of action, someone who could handle a situation when it was teetering on the brink of chaos. The man before him was his current meal ticket and he'd be damned to see a good situation turn sour from any lack of action on his part.

"Damn them all to hell," Soapy muttered again, his words came out in a jagged burst of breath as he kicked the remnants of a shattered chair into the corner, sending a cloud of dust into the air.

"Well, hell, Soapy," Jack drawled, his Texan accent as thick as ever, "I don't reckon this place is gonna clean itself up. Maybe you wanna cool down for a spell?"

Soapy's glare shifted to Jack, his nostrils flaring with each breath. For a long moment, he said nothing, standing still, his fists still clenched at his sides. The rage that had consumed him seemed to hang in the air, thick and suffocating. He just closed his eyes for a moment, breathing deeply, trying to regain control.

"You're right," Soapy muttered, his voice tight. "I need to think. But damn it, Jack. What they did to me down there? I can't let it go. I won't let it go."

Texas Jack approached slowly, his hands resting casually on his hips. He had no intention of rushing in; he knew better than to jump into the fray without thinking. He studied Soapy's face, the hard lines around his eyes, the clenched jaw and fists. His friend's rage had boiled over and Jack could see the man was still teetering between full-blown rage and the calculating mind that made him so dangerous.

"Listen, Soap," Jack said softly, his voice steady but with an undercurrent of authority. "I know what happened down there wasn't pretty. But losing your head ain't gonna do us any good. Think this through. We need to figure out our next move."

Soapy's eyes snapped open, and for a moment, the fire in them flared again. "Next move?" he snarled. "Take out every single damn Mountie in this town. Starting with Grant. How about that?"

Texas Jack took a step forward, raising a hand to calm him down. "Easy,"

Soapy's lips twisted into a sneer, but the heat in his eyes had cooled just slightly. "Don't you manage me. He thinks he's better than me, Jack. I'll show him just how wrong he is."

"Grant's nothing but a nuisance," Jack offered. "A dangerous nuisance, but only a nuisance. Let's not make him a problem. We don't need to give the Mounties any more reason to come after us."

There was a long silence, and then Soapy's shoulders dropped, a weary sigh escaping him. He wiped a hand over his face, the fury momentarily ebbing away as Jack's words sank in. Soapy wasn't a man to back down easily, but he wasn't stupid either.

"Is there any booze left in here, or did you smash everything?"

"Whiskey's in the desk," Soap said, his voice gruff.

With a squeal of swollen wood on wood, Texas Jack opened one of the desk's drawers and retrieved the bottle. He handed it to Soapy. After his boss removed the cork, threw it away and took a long swing from the bottle, Jack held up a cigar.

"Have a smoke and let's think this through."

Soapy took a deep breath and then nodded, accepting the cheroot and lighting it with an ornate gold lighter he retrieved from his waistcoat.

"Let the bounty do its work," Jack said simply, his eyes steady. "Sit back and let that drama play itself out. In the meantime, we go about our business. The usual capers. Run the town, make our money. You've got enough on your plate already, Soapy."

Soapy took a long puff of his cigar, exhaling slowly, still chewing over Jack's words. The idea didn't sit right at first, but maybe Jack was right, the key was not to chase Grant directly but let the chaos and competition destroy him for them.

"Alright, Jack. We'll play it your way. But we don't forget. The clock's ticking. If the bounty doesn't work, then we'll take what I want and do it ourselves."

Jack's grin widened. "There you go. Not everything has to be loud and messy. Sometimes, the quietest moves make the biggest waves."

Soapy took a deep pull from his cigar, letting the smoke roll out slowly. "Yeah, yeah. Quiet's all well and good. But there's always room for a little excitement in the mix. Can't just sit around all day with my feet up. There's got to be some action, Jack."

Texas Jack chuckled and in his smooth voice suggested, "What about trying something new?"

"What mischief are you coming up with now?"

"The merchants, the shops, the docks," Jack said, his eyes gleamed with a dangerous spark that was all too familiar to Soapy. "Let's make them think they need our protection. We convince them to part with their money for the 'safety' of their goods. 'A little insurance,' as they say. We'll help 'em sleep better at night, for a price."

Soapy leaned forward, intrigued by the idea. "Protection rackets? That could work."

Jack nodded, his voice cool and calculated. “We start with the smaller merchants. Offer them ‘protection’ from the local troublemakers. A little whisper here, a little sabotage there, a predictable fire over there? Then, they’ll start seeing us as the ‘saviours.’ And when the time’s right, we take a cut of everything they’ve got.”

Soapy took a long drag from his cigar, staring into its smouldering tip as if it could divine for him the answers he was searching for. The grin on his face widened, and he said, “I like it. That’s an idea I can get behind. As I’ve always said, there’s plenty of ways to make a dollar in Skagway, and the best kind of dollar is one earned out of someone else’s pocket.”

CHAPTER XVIII

The Next Task

Standing at the threshold of the warehouse, the worn floorboards of the pier the building sat on creaked underneath Grant's tall black riding boots. The scene before him was, as promised, overwhelming. Stacks upon stacks, upon stacks of canvas dunnage bags were piled higher than he cared to count. He had thought the baggage holding the territory's customs duties had been a significant pile to manage. This was something on a scale he had no real way to rationalize or comprehend. Staff Sergeant Hyles had been right, words did not do the scenario any justice. It was something that indeed had to been seen to be understood.

The air inside the cavernous warehouse was thick with the scent of aged wood, mildew, rot and the mustiness of old, damp paper. It was a chaotic jumble. Crates and bags filled every corner and most of the square footage between them. Everywhere he looked, there was some sort of delivery: boxes wrapped in brown paper, bags that bulged or split open bags that had disgorged piles of letters over the damp floor. It was an unholy mess, one that seemed almost impossible to manage.

As his eyes scanned the mountain of mail, a frown creased his forehead. He'd seen disorganized chaos before but this? This was different. The sheer volume of it took him by surprise. Skagway wasn't just a staging point, it was a chokepoint. Every letter, every package, every communication destined for those who had entered Canada in the past year of the gold rush was in here, waiting, clamouring to be moved out and delivered.

Hyles stood beside Grant, arms crossed, watching the Constable's face as he processed what he was seeing and working through the problem. The vastness of it was staggering, but it wasn't the size of the task that bothered him most, it was the urgency. This mail had to move. People depended on it. Delays here weren't just inconvenience; they were a bottleneck that could cripple the entire Klondike territory from British Columbia to the Yukon and beyond. If they couldn't get this sorted, everything could grind to a halt.

Grant let out a low whistle, shaking his head as he took in the cluttered scene.

"I know, right?" Hyles agreed.

"Yeah, damn," Grant finally said, his voice steady despite the turmoil in his thoughts. "Moving all of this over the mountains?"

They made their way deeper into the warehouse, weaving through the piles of crates and bundles of letters. Inside his uniform jacket, Grant could feel his pocket watch ticking against his chest, and with each count of its movement, the situation would worsen and complicate itself further. He knew that the pressure was only going to mount until they could clear the backlog. He wasn't sure what the answer was yet, but he knew that movement, of any kind, was vital.

At the far end of the warehouse, near another set of doors, Grant spotted his friend Jorge. The long rider was speaking with a couple of dockhands, gesturing toward the various crates, his face set in a grim line. When he saw Grant and Hyles approaching, he gave a short nod and waved them over. Through these rear doors, a slight breeze carried the scent of saltwater, timber and something more unpleasant, wharves often featured that.

"You made it Amigo," Jorge said, his voice calm but with an underlying edge of frustration. Grant offered a quick nod and shook Jorge's hand firmly. The Mexican didn't wait for him to respond, saying, "Welcome to the mess. I'm not sure how to handle all of this. I don't know whether to thank you or shoot you."

"If it's shoot me, you had better get in line," Grant quipped.

"I heard about that, and I am sorry; but, amigo-amigo, this is terrible. Every ship brings more, more, more."

"What would you suggest?" Grant asked.

"A fire would be a good start," Jorge suggested and perhaps not entirely in jest.

"That's not helpful," Hyles shot back.

"From your position, or mine?" Jorge replied. "For me, it solves many things. I don't need this job, Grant asked me for help, he's the only reason I am here."

"I appreciate your help and insights," Grant said, hoping to apply some diplomatic salve to this open wound before it became septic. "We're all looking for a solution here Sergeant. Jorge runs freighting in the Klondike, and I value his opinion: humour and all."

"It has to move," Jorge observed, "That's the most important thing, move as much of this out before the next ship dumps another load on the dock."

"I agree," Grant said. "The faster we can move it the better."

Hyles shot him a sceptical look, "How exactly do you plan on doing that?"

Grant didn't hesitate. "We use both passes. Chilkoot might be the best for the bulk and White Pass for the lighter, urgent materials. We'll need to keep things moving constantly, with no delays."

Hyles needed more, and he pressed Grant, "No delays is a big ask out here. We also need to plan for the long-term, this isn't just about moving the current mail. We need a way to handle future shipments. Otherwise, we'll be right back here in no time, facing the same problem."

"Moving this first is key, that will allow space to sort through the new arrivals and get those on the move as well."

"Yes, but we need a system," Hyles said. "A regular schedule, some kind of oversight. What about once it gets to Yukon?"

"One thing at a time Sergeant," Grant replied, rubbing his temples as he worked through the forest of options and challenges that popped up with every new thought or idea.

"What about security?" Hyles asked. "We can't just have men wander through the pass carrying sacks of letters without some form of protection."

"Agreed," Grant said.

"What about here?" Jorge asked. "There's theft actively underway."

"Do we know that?" Grant asked.

"It's Skagway, of course there's theft," an exasperated Hyles replied. "My men have tried but there's only three of us. They were up all last night. The minute they leave, the light fingers reappear."

"There are men here who've been less than honest," Jorge agreed, his voice dropping to a lower tone. "If we can't secure this, we're going to lose a lot more than just time."

"We hire guards to keep watch and stop the theft," Grant said. "Sergeant, if you can focus on security, Jorge and I will work on routes and getting all of this out of here as soon as possible. One thing at a time. We need to start, the rest we can address as it happens. If we don't begin somewhere we become paralysed."

"How are we paying them?" Hyles asked.

"Cash and coin, on the barrelhead," replied Grant. "Don't worry about it, we can talk more back at the office."

Hyles gave a brief nod in agreement.

"Alright," Grant said, and turned to Jorge. "We've got a lot of work ahead of us."

The pressure was on, if they didn't get the mail secured and sent out, the entire system could collapse. Grant wasn't one to back down from a challenge. He was already planning the next steps, determined to get the job done right. They had no choice but to succeed.

After Hyles stomped off to address hiring security for the warehouse, Jorge and Grant walked amongst the piled mail, surveying the sheer volume of material they needed to move.

"We can't handle all of this on our own," Grant said. "We'll need to coordinate with the freighter companies on both sides of the mountains."

"I know some of the operators, but it's going to take time," Jorge admitted.

"It's going to be best that we do it underway," Grant offered. "If you take the Chilkoot; I'll take White Pass. We meet in Bennett and then handle the sorting there. Meanwhile, Hyles handles sorting any new mail into the batches that will go over the Chilkoot route or the White Pass route."

"Until they build that railway over the White Pass, it's a start."

"The railway would be a big help," Grant mused. "Until then, the Chilkoot should take the bulk of the volume. Boats from here to Dyea. We use the freighters operating between Dyea and the tramways. Then from Sheep Camp swing it all over the border using the tramway; and from there: the local freighters can carry the loads from Crater Lake to Bennett."

"It's more established on that side, yes," Jorge agreed.

"Fewer delays than using the Dead Horse Trail, I'll wager. We take advantage of these companies and their systems. Once they drop off one shipment, they return for the next one. We both make our crossings, and we'll meet back in Bennett and see what's worked."

"It is the beginning of a plan amigo," Jorge said. "I'll start making arrangements."

"Thank you, Jorge," Grant said.

"Don't thank me yet, we haven't agreed on my fee." Jorge shot back over his shoulder as he strode out of the warehouse.

Standing at the main doors, Grant looked out over the port of Skagway, his mind frenetically mapping out the details. The sheer scale of what lay ahead was daunting. Sergeant Hyles was right. It wasn't just about delivering the mail, or moving just this heap of post, it would require the creation of a sustainable process to keep the flow of information moving. As the Klondike grew and demand increased, Skagway was just the starting point.

CHAPTER XIX

The Second Attempt

The late afternoon sun hung low over Skagway, casting a golden hue over the narrow streets. The sky was clear, the mountains loomed in the distance, the light on their jagged peaks a reminder of the ruggedness of the Alaskan wilderness. The streets were filled with the usual hustle and bustle of this: the metropolis of Alaska. Prospectors, traders, and drifters moved through the narrow lanes between the various saloons, general stores and hotels.

As Grant walked along Broadway Street, his eyes moved constantly from one side to the other, scanning the crowd for any sign of trouble. His mind was preoccupied with the next critical stages of moving the accumulated post and mail out of town, over the mountains and into the Klondike. In his opinion, the task was far from even started. While his thoughts lingered on the logistics of his challenge, there was something else gnawing at him, something instinctive, a feeling that he couldn't shake.

At first, it was subtle. A shift in the crowd. A flicker of movement out of the corner of his eye. He didn't immediately turn to see it, he wouldn't allow himself to be distracted. But as he walked on, the feeling of eyes on him grew. It was different than the anxious fears that had percolated around his mind before. This was an actuality, and it wasn't just one person, no, that would have been too obvious. There was a pattern to this feeling. A subtle shift in the people around him, like the way the wind moves through dry grass before a storm hits.

Grant's steps slowed imperceptibly, and his hand, almost instinctively, brushed the outer flap of the holster on his hip. He didn't turn around. He had not fully determined if it was just a new paranoia creeping in; or, if someone was genuinely tailing him.

The alleyways here were narrow, cramped between the buildings that jutted out into the street, their weathered facades standing close together like old men gossiping. He kept his pace steady, his expression neutral. He had learned not to betray any sense of alarm. If someone was following him, they had to make the first move.

And yet, the feeling refused to go away.

A soft shuffle behind him, a boot, scraping against the dirt ended all further thoughts about postal service. The sound was familiar, but not too soft to be heard over the other sounds of Skagway. A cart rattled by. A series of shouts from a nearby vendor. The whinny of a passing horse. It stood out to him all the same and now he didn't need to turn around to confirm that someone was following him.

Grant's eyes flicked across the street casually, searching the crowd. He noticed a group of prospectors talking near a saloon entrance, their faces ruddy from the sun, their voices low. He scanned the faces of the men lingering in the shadows, the women huddled near the doorways, but none of them seemed to be paying him any undue or special attention.

The crowd around him seemed to swell and contract, each passerby moving as if they were part of some strange, unwritten choreography. The tension in the air grew thicker, and Grant's senses sharpened. Every movement felt too deliberate. Every shadow too deep. He kept his back straight, his posture confident, but every few seconds, his gaze flicked to the edges of the street, checking the corners of his vision for threats.

He passed a saloon where a couple of men were arguing over a hand of cards. Grant didn't even glance in their direction. He kept moving and the closer he got to the intersection ahead, the more he began to feel the weight of the eyes on him, the awareness crawling up his spine like a cold, invisible hand.

A shop's door slammed closed behind him, just loud enough to make him flinch. His heart skipped a beat, but he didn't dare react. Arriving at the intersection, Grant played the role of newcomer, stopping and looking around to get his bearings before continuing on his way. That's when Grant saw his pursuer. He was no longer just a shadow.

He was taller than most, with dark hair and a long, weather-beaten coat. He was casually standing just outside a small shop, as if he were simply another citizen of the town. Grant's sharp eyes picked out the details, the shuffle as the man had stopped following and pretended instead to be waiting outside the building, the way the man's hand was too close to the revolver on his hip, the slight movement of his head as he deliberately tracked Grant's every step.

Grant's instincts tightened, and he forced himself to look away, to maintain the illusion of indifference. Every further step he took confirmed what he feared: he was being followed, but by how many?

At first, it had seemed like a coincidence, but Grant knew better than to trust that feeling. The man wasn't just walking in the same direction. He was deliberately straying behind him, just far enough to avoid detection. Grant's lips tightened. This wasn't a coincidence or an accidental meeting.

He continued walking, forcing himself not to quicken his pace. The last thing he wanted was to show any weakness. Still, his thoughts raced as he moved through the streets. It seemed like the man was playing the long game, he was waiting, watching, looking for the right moment to strike. Grant had no intention of allowing him that moment.

Grant could feel more than one set of eyes on him, his instincts screaming that the attack wasn't just a possibility, it was an inevitability. Even though Wood had counselled him to leave town the moment it became too dangerous, he couldn't just disappear into the wilderness, not with the Mounties counting on him. And so, he continued to walk, focused on keeping his movements calm and measured.

There was no way to escape on the street and the detachment's office was still a few blocks away. If he wanted to break this tail, he had to try something now. Grant veered towards an alleyway on his left, a narrow passageway between two storefronts. It was a gamble, but if he could cut over by a street and break their sight line, he hoped to slip away.

He turned the corner, and stepped into the alley, passing an elderly woman sweeping the front porch of one shop. He glanced over his shoulder, his pace quickening as the walls of the alley closed in. Shadowed from the low sun and isolating him from the sounds of the street behind, his boots crunched softly against the gravel. The hairs on the back of his neck stood on end, and the rhythm of his pulse beating in his ears intensified as he walked deeper into the shadows.

Reaching the end of the building, in the moment he rounded the corner his heart skipped its steady beat. The alley didn't continue to the next street. It stopped in a dead end.

He cursed under his breath.

There was no way out. The only option now was to turn back, but he already knew that whoever was trailing him had likely caught on. He took a step back, eyes scanning the entrance, calculating his options. His breath caught in his throat as he saw a figure at the far end of the alley, blocking his only exit. Tall, broad-shouldered, it was the man who had been following him.

Before Grant could react, two more men appeared behind the first, cutting off the exit to the alley entirely. The odds had just shifted dramatically, and now he found himself surrounded.

For the first time since entering the alley, Grant's hand went to his holster, but before he could draw, the trio had brandished their own weapons. The first man drew out a gleaming knife. The steel flashed before it entered the dim light of the alley. The two men on either side of him showed Grant their revolvers were already in hand. The savage gleam in lead man's eyes locked on to Grant's.

"You should've known better than to turn into a corner, Mountie," he sneered. "You're out of options now."

"You here for Soapy's bounty?" Grant challenged him.

"Damn right. The name's Rourke and I'm gonna deliver you straight to hell. You can tell the devil I sent you."

Grant's pulse raced as he assessed the situation. The three men were rough, imposing and no strangers to violence. A knife and no easy way out. He could draw his revolver and try to shoot his way out, but in such close quarters, he might end up catching bullets and a blade in his gut.

A sickening grin spread across Rourke's face as he took a step forward, the knife held low but ready. “Time to die.”

Grant didn’t respond. He needed a distraction, something to give him a moment of leverage. As Rourke moved closer, knife in hand, Grant shifted his weight, eyes darting between the three men, mentally mapping out the movements of his attackers. Rourke was the immediate threat. The two goons were larger, slower and less coordinated but held guns. He had to bet on them only being here to contain him for Rourke, rather than delivering the kill shot in this claustrophobic nightmare.

First, he needed to survive long enough to make his move. He began to slowly backpedal towards the end of the building and where the alley turned. As he did, Rourke began to advance with the two goons following.

Rourke lunged forward, the knife hissing through the air.

Grant dodged the slash easily. His heart thudded in his chest as he twisted away and continued to edge himself backwards, further away from the street.

Rourke snarled and came at Grant again, the outlaw’s body moving with the agility of someone who had spent years in this kind of fight. The knife stabbed forward, aiming for Grant’s gut, but he was ready. He sidestepped, grabbing Rourke’s wrist and twisting, used the man’s momentum against him. The knife clattered to the ground. He threw a solid jab across Rourke’s jaw and backed away again.

Fury flashed in Rourke’s eyes. “Not bad, Grant,” he spat, voice thick with venom as he retrieved his knife from the ground. “But this isn’t over.”

“Come on big man,” Grant taunted him. “Third time’s the charm.”

Rourke advanced again, swinging the knife through the air in a brutal arc towards Grant’s face. The Mountie ducked under the slash and lunged forward, slamming his shoulder into the man’s midsection, lifting him into a brutal tackle that sent both men crashing to the ground in a heap.

The two goons, their revolvers raised and could have ended Grant with ease. Instead, they watched as he and Rourke fought. His gamble was paying off, for now, and so he became focused entirely on Rourke. In the narrow space of the alley, Grant's fists slammed into Rourke's ribs and face, forcing the man back for a moment. Rourke was tough and absorbed the blows without complaint, and with a quick thrust the knife once again came at Grant aiming for his midsection.

Grant pushed the blade away and scrambled back to his feet. The knife had come too close. He had no choice but to keep moving. With a grunt, he shoved Rourke's head against the wall of the alley with a sickening thud, momentarily stunning him. Grant didn't waste time. In the same fluid motion, he pivoted and ducked around the bend in the alley, using the corner to put some distance between him and his attackers.

Drawing his Adams revolver from its holster, he turned, planted his feet and held his breath. He leant out around the corner, aimed at the broad chest of one of the goons and pulled the trigger. He fired once, twice, the punching echoes of his shots pummelled his ears in the confined space of the alley.

Rourke was just getting to his feet as Grant's shots caught one his goons in their centre mass. The man dropped, lifeless, to the gravel and muddy floor of the alley with a damp thud. The other gunman cursed and fired back, his wild shot slamming into the wall behind the Mountie, high and wide from its target but forcing Grant to duck back behind the corner.

Rourke called out, "You're slippery, I'll give you that." The Outlaw's heartless laugh was menacing, "There's no getting away. You've been a real pain in Soapy's side. I'm gonna fix that now, once and for all."

Grant could hear the scrape of metal on gravel, which he presumed was Rourke retrieving the dead goon's gun.

Boxed in, with two gunfighters to neutralize, Grant knew he was in a bad position. One of them could pin him down with covering fire while the other walked up and cooly shot him in the head. With a steady hand, Grant pulled the two spent shells out of his revolver's cylinder and replaced them with two fresh cartridges. Years of drill and practice, for him, made the often-overlooked task of reloading on the fly a simple one. He snapped the cylinder closed as he backed himself to the very end of the alleyway and took up a position behind an old wooden crate.

Finger on the trigger and his back to the wall, as a last stand went, he thought this had to fit the definition.

When Rourke and the other goon charged around the corner, the first shots they fired were undisciplined and ragged. Rourke peeled out wide to the left, hugging the far wall of the alley.

Crouched low by the edge of the crate, Grant's aim was steady and his return fire accurate. Next to Rourke, the other gunman's eyes widened in surprise, and he staggered as the first of Grant's shots caught him high in the right shoulder. The bullet spun him back and before he could react, another bullet tore through the right side of his chest, straight into his heart. As the revolver fell from his hand and skidded across the ground, he dropped like a stone, forcing Rourke up against the wall

Rourke was tripped up by the corpse but managed to fire another round in Grant's direction.

As Grant adjusted his aim, a commanding voice boomed down the alleyway from the street, "Drop the gun! Stand down!"

Rourke twisted to look towards the shout and began to raise his gun when a pair of rifle shots rang out. The shots both landed well, driving the outlaw back against the wall. His limp body slid down the wall to crumple to the alley floor next to the other goon.

Grant blinked, his mind wholly absorbed by its flight-or-fight response. His heart was pounding, and his breaths were ragged.

"Whoever's back there, come on out," the commanding voice's deep baritone called out once more. "You hearing me?"

"I hear you," Grant answered. "I'm coming out."

"Keep your hands where we can see 'em. If you don't shoot us, we won't shoot you."

"I'm holstering my weapon," Grant assured the voice.

"That's fine, come on out now," the voice ordered.

Grant reached his hands out in front of himself as he turned the corner of the alleyway, he splayed his fingers open to show he wasn't concealing anything. As he stepped over the bodies of Rourke and the other goon he looked towards the alleyway's entrance. There, standing tall and imposing were three soldiers. They wore the distinctive blue coats of the U.S. Army and broad-brimmed, high-crowned campaign hats. On either side of the

Sergeant were two Privates, their rifles raised and held with steady aim, the smoke still curling from the barrels.

"Step away from them, and approach," the commanding voice, belonging to the Sergeant, instructed Grant.

One of the Privates, observed, "He's one of them Mounties. I told you so, Baker."

"Quiet," the Sergeant barked.

As Grant approached, he stepped over the body of the first goon he had shot. Emerging back into a patch of low sunlight, it revealed that his three saviours were African Americans. Grant realized they must be the Buffalo Soldiers of the 24th Infantry. He had heard about the all-black regiments before but had not realized they were stationed as far off as Alaska.

"You alright there, Mister?" The Sergeant asked.

"I will be. I'm Constable Grant of the North-West Mounted Police. I'm in your debt, Sergeant."

"Told ya!" The Private said again.

Grant's body still hummed with the adrenaline of the fight, but he allowed himself a breath. "Thank you," he said, his voice still rough from the struggle.

"Sergeant Walters, 24th Infantry, 'L' Company. This is Private Baker, the chatty one is Hill. He's the one who saw these three follow you off the street," The Sergeant replied. "Once we heard the gunshots? Well, you know the rest. It's all over now. Did you know these men?"

"No, I don't. They work for Soapy Smith."

"Not anymore they don't," Private Hill quipped.

"You and Baker go secure the entrance, we don't need any of these lookey-loos coming back here before the Sheriff arrives," Walters ordered Hill.

"Yes, Sergeant." The wiry little Private replied. He and Baker both turned on their heels and strode back to the alley's entrance. Grant could see a group of onlookers had been growing out on the street, jostling with each other to get a view of what had happened.

"Get back, all of you," the larger Baker, his voice firm and calm, commanded the crowd as they approached it. "Move back!"

Walters looked at the bodies laid out in the alleyway, "This sort of thing happen often with you?"

"I have to admit, it's become more frequent in recent days."

"Lucky you," Walters snorted.

"I'm starting to think luck's the only thing keeping me alive lately," Grant mused before asking, "How long have you been in Skagway?"

"Not long, a little over a week? We're just an advance party. Scouting out the place. Captain Hovey and the rest of the Company will follow later this year looks like. We'll be posting up in Dyea, I think."

"Dyea's better, keeps you out of this sort of work," Grant replied.

"You got that right," Walter said. "The Sheriffs can have it. Speaking of which, what are you Mounties doing here? Canada's that-a-way."

"I'm here to sort out the post, our mail, that needs to get to the Klondike."

"That's a policeman's job?"

"Exactly what I thought at first, but yes."

"Soapy Smith's after you because of the mail?"

"No, I've cost him money, stopped some capers and killed his men. Doing the job, that's why he wants me dead."

"Doing the job," Walters repeated. "Yeah, I get that."

"There's a bounty on my head. Two thousand."

Walters whistled, "Hoo, lord. That would do it."

"You want to collect?" Grant joked.

"Naw, I'm good Constable, seems you can handle yourself, but maybe in future you shouldn't be travelling all on your lonesome?"

"You make a fair point," Grant admitted. "In that case, would I be able to impose on you and your men for a small favour?"

CHAPTER XX

The Confrontation

After Grant pushed open the front door to Jeff Smith's Parlor, the piano's jaunty tune stopped, cutting off the carefree melody with a sharp finality. The low hum of conversation stilled, replaced by the soft scrape of chairs against the wooden floor and the sound of boots shifting nervously. Someone coughed.

The atmosphere in the saloon had abruptly shifted. A ripple of tension spread through the room as the door banged shut behind Grant. His boots echoed on the floorboards as he moved further inside the narrow space. The dim light of early evening filtered through the grimy windows leaving long slanting shadows that spilled across the room, their darkness making the faces of the men and women inside seem more drawn, more suspicious. Drifters, gamblers, merchants, and prospectors, all drawn like moths to the friction in the air, their eyes rested on the Parlor's new arrivals. The moment had become a showdown, before anyone had even said a word.

Sergeant Walters and the two other Buffalo Soldiers stood behind Grant, the heavy tread of their boots coming to attention cut through the silence. Dressed in their faded blue Army uniform jackets, their faces were grim and resolute below the Montana Peaks of their campaign hats. They oozed with the confidence of men who had survived far worse than what Skagway could throw at them. Though the room was full of rough men, the patrons all seemed to shrink in the face of Grant's arrival with the Buffalo Soldiers flanking him.

Behind the bar, the bartender stared at them with disdain. His gaze flicked between Grant and the soldiers. When he spoke, his voice was laced with an unmistakable hostility, "We don't serve their kind," the bartender said, his words carrying the weight of centuries of prejudice. "You best turn around and leave."

Grant's expression remained cold. The way the bartender had said it was enough to make his blood simmer, though he kept it in check. He wasn't here to start a fight with the man behind the bar, his fight was with the man's boss. However, he wasn't about to let a comment like that slide either.

He fixed the bartender with a look that didn't leave room for any doubt, "What, soldiers?"

The bartender's sneer deepened, but he didn't speak immediately. Instead, his eyes darted over to the far side of the room, where men were gathered in the shadowed corners, watching the interaction with interest.

Grant stood firm, his hand casually resting on his holster, a stance that sent a subtle warning to anyone paying attention. The rifle carrying Buffalo Soldiers who flanked him appeared equally unyielding.

"Is there a problem?" Sergeant Walters' voice rumbled from behind Grant, his tone level but carrying a quiet menace that was impossible to ignore.

The bartender stiffened, caught between his personal prejudices and the unmistakable weight of the soldiers' presence. He hesitated, then looked toward the men at the back wall again, as though waiting for a signal. It was clear the bartender wasn't about to start anything openly.

"You don't belong here," the bartender muttered, though his voice lacked the conviction of his earlier words.

Grant took a step forward, eyes never leaving the man's face. "Maybe so, but here we are all the same." He paused, letting the weight of his words sink in before continuing, his voice steady but it held an undeniable edge.

The bartender's face flushed, but before he could respond, a door creaked open at the rear of the Parlor. The well-tailored blue suit of Soapy Smith appeared, his immaculate presence immediately commanded attention. His sharp eyes, shadowed beneath a wide-brimmed hat, scanned the room, and for a moment, it felt as if the entire bar was holding its breath. When his gaze landed on Grant, Soapy's lips curled into a thin, almost imperceptible smile behind his beard.

"Well, well, if it isn't the Royal Canadian Cavalry," Soapy's voice was smooth, almost too smooth. "Or is it the postal service now? I can't recall." He took a step forward, his boots clicking sharply against the floor, "I was wondering if you'd have the courage to show your face around here."

Grant said nothing, though the tension of the situation spread across his shoulders. This was no casual meeting. For the Mountie, anything less than a full confrontation would be a disappointment, and he was prepared for whatever came next.

The people in the saloon took their cue from Soapy, their eyes tracking his every movement in silent expectation. No one dared to speak, Soapy had ruled this town for long enough that everyone knew better than to cross the man in his own joint. What this Mountie was doing flew in the face of that unspoken rule. The patrons waited with bated breath for Soapy to lay out the rules of this engagement.

Here, in the heart of Soapy's empire, Grant knew he had to challenge the gangster's power. The man was a master manipulator, who had woven his influence into the very fabric of Skagway. From Grant's perspective, it was time for that influence to end.

The Constable steeled his own voice, when he said, "You failed, Soapy, again. Your man Rourke is dead. I thought I'd let you know sooner rather than later."

"Rourke? Never heard of him," was Smith's dismissive reply. "What did he do to earn such a fate?"

"He tried to collect on your bounty. Anyone else tries to collect? They'll meet the same end. Like Rourke, like Milton and like McCade."

"Big talk from a little, red-coated man," Smith replied. "Is that why you brought the blue jackets along?"

Soapy rapped his knuckles on the bar. The barkeep swiftly set out a glass and a bottle of whiskey for his boss. He uncorked the bottle and poured a measure of the amber liquid into the glass.

"You've got some nerve, Grant," Soapy said, his voice smooth as velvet. He raised the glass and took a leisurely sip. He looked over the trio of Buffalo soldiers. There was no fear in his gaze, only the disconcerting confidence that made him dangerous. The threatening nature of his voice was unmistakable, “I half expected for you to come in guns blazing, but this? This is, quite the surprise. What am I supposed to infer from the presence of your coloured friends?”

Grant’s eyes considered Soapy with measured disdain, “Infer whatever you like. Just know that I’m not afraid of you or your bounty.”

Soapy’s smile stretched a little wider, the look on his face almost one of pity. “I see it now. You’re just a regular, beef-headed Gump who just don’t know better. You should be afraid.” He chuckled, the sound a low rumble of amusement. He tipped his hat back slightly, revealing more of his sharp features as he continued, “Stupider men than you have known that. What’s your plan, huh? You think you can waltz in here and push me around like I’m some two-bit crook?”

“You think you’re untouchable?” Grant didn’t flinch and his voice was a low growl now, one that seemed to echo in the otherwise quiet room. “You think because you’ve been running this town like it’s your personal playground that you’ve earned some kind of invincibility?”

The tension between them was stacked like dry kindling waiting for the right spark.

Soapy’s eyes flashed, his teeth showing in a tight grin. “In this town, I am invincible,” he said, his voice like ice. “Everyone knows that. Hell, most are too scared to even look me in the eye. But you? You’re here because you’re either a fool or you’ve got something to prove. Right now, I’m thinking it’s a little of both.”

Grant mirrored Soapy and made his voice smooth, when he replied, “It’s funny, when I first heard about you, I thought I’d end up meeting a man of substance. Someone who would present a challenge. A proper adversary.” He let the words hang in the air for a moment, then smiled, “It turns out, you’re more of a sideshow carnival act than anything else. All bluster and no show.”

Soapy’s lips twitched upward, but it was more of a grimace than a smile. He adjusted the brim of his hat, eyes never leaving

Grant's. "You sure do like to talk a lot. Is that your strategy? Boring me to death until I can't take it anymore?"

"You're not the first snake oil salesman I've had to deal with, and your tricks are far from remarkable."

Soapy gave a soft snort, as if Grant's words were too light to even phase him. He finished his whiskey and set the glass on the bar. Taking slow steps forward, he began narrowing the space between them as he spoke, "I've seen men like you come and go. Ones who thought they could stand up to me. Not one of them managed to last, not one managed to take me down or keep breathing air."

"Is that so? Here I am, and I'm calling your bluff."

"Call my bluff?" Soapy said, chuckling under his breath, "I'm not playing cards, Grant. But if I was, you'd be out of luck. I'm the one holding all the aces. You know that don't you?" He inclined his head towards the men against the back wall, his hired goons and henchmen. They were a solid wall of muscle, their eyes cold, faces unreadable as they watched, weapons waiting to be invited to join in.

Grant didn't flinch. He knew their presence was a silent threat, but he wasn't concerned. Not now. "Aces, huh? And how many of them did you hide up your sleeve?" He leaned in just a little, his voice dropping low. "Cheating's not winning, but a dirty, rotten slack-jawed grifter like you wouldn't understand that."

The stillness that followed was thick, the kind of silence that hangs just before the storm. Then, in an instant, everything seemed to happen at once.

The cluster of men along the back wall all stood up with alarming speed. They weren't just thugs; these were men with experience, the kind who knew how to handle a confrontation. As they reached for their revolvers, the Buffalo Soldiers were already reacting, their rifles raised and aimed in an instant. The room became a blur of motion and sound, gruff voices, chairs scraping, the telltale clicks of weapons being drawn and hammers cocked.

Soapy's smile faded, replaced by a cold glare that sent a chill through the room. Grant stood his ground. The two men locked eyes, each sizing the other up. The room seemed to draw a collective breath, waiting for something to happen.

"Did McCade give you that scar, or did you cut yourself shaving?" When Grant did not reply, the gangster scoffed. "I thought so. You know Grant, I almost feel sorry for you," Soapy said, like a predator sizing up its prey, his eyes glittering with amusement, his lip twitching into a smirk. "You're out of your depth. This little crusade of yours ain't going to end the way you think."

"How about we agree to disagree?" Grant offered.

"Probably best it goes that way. You have no jurisdiction and you're boring me now," Soapy said, his breath heavy with whiskey and smoke. He dragged a finger down the side of his own face, mimicking Grant's scar. "Unless you want to get a matching mark to balance out yourself out, I think it's time for you to go."

Grant's face was a mask of resolve. He stood firm, arms at his sides, facing Soapy head-on.

Walters spoke up, his rifle's aim unwavering, "Unless there's something else to be said, I think we're done here, Grant."

"Why don't you listen to your pet soldier?" Soapy mocked, "Show's over for tonight. You're a good man, Grant. Too good for this world, I think." He turned his back on Grant, returned to the bar and poured himself another drink.

"Time to go," Walters said over Grant's shoulder.

The Constable nodded. There was nothing left to say. He had stood his ground, but there was no denying that for all the sharp barbs he had thrown, for all the bravado he had tried to summon, it had barely made a dent in Soapy Smith's armour. He was still standing, confident and unflinching. He could feel the blood rushing to his head, the frustration boiling up inside of him.

"Keep running your carny act, Soapy. Just remember that sooner or later, everyone grows tired of a clown in a big hat."

As Grant and the Buffalo soldiers backed their way to the Parlor's door, Soapy turned to watch them leave. He offered a small wave, and replied, "Thanks for stopping by. Next time, don't bring the help with you." The gangster's voice added a final warning as they exited the building, "We're not done yet, Mountie. I'll see to that."

CHAPTER XXI

The Growing Conflict

"Where are we headed?" Sergeant Walters asked as they moved through the streets Skagway.

Grant replied. "Our detachment has an office a couple of blocks away. I need to check in with them."

Walters nodded. "We'll escort you there. After that little performance? It's best you get indoors for a spell."

While the four men made their way through the heart of Skagway, the soldiers stayed close, their rifles slung over their backs but ready for action at any moment. Grant was grateful for their company, as the feeling of impending danger in his chest only grew. He was caught between two worlds: his duty to the Mounties and the ever-present threat of Soapy's revenge.

"Did that go as you hoped?" Private Hill asked Grant.

"No. If I'm being honest, other than showing him I'm still alive, I'm not sure what I had hoped for."

"You did that," the Private quipped. "I don't think he's ever been cussed out like that. And, in his own joint? Shit."

"Private," Walters growled in warning.

"What? I'm just saying, the man did what he wanted to do."

"Almost got us shot for it too," Private Baker offered.

"I am sorry for that," Grant offered. "You three have already done more than enough. I put you all at risk."

"Getting shot is in our job description," Private Baker replied.

"Hell, it is the job description!" Private Hill added. "It was worth it seeing that gangster's eyes light up when you called him a card sharp. Lord, I wouldn't have missed that for nothing!"

All four of them laughed at the observation and Grant felt a slight weight lift off his shoulders. The situation was dire, but with allies like these, he knew he might just stand a chance.

When they arrived outside the detachment's office, Sergeant Hyles emerged onto the street, his rifle up and at the ready, along with a very worried Jorge.

"Grant! Are you alright?" Hyles asked, looking over the three Buffalo soldiers as he approached them.

"Yes, thanks to these gentlemen." Grant replied.

Jorge was next to speak, "We heard a Mountie got shot."

"Shot at," Grant replied. "I was shot at."

"Sergeant, the Mounted Police thanks you and your men," Hyles said.

"We were happy to be of assistance," Sergeant Walters replied. "Grant had already done most of the work by the time we showed up." Private Baker added. "We just helped with the cleaning up."

"Bounty chasers?" Hyles asked.

"Yeah, some of Soapy's guys." Grant replied.

"What happened to them?" Jorge asked.

"What do think happened to them?" Private Hill joked.

"You're not to walk the streets unescorted from this point forward." Hyles ordered Grant.

"It will be fine, really" Grant protested.

"That's an order, Constable. I'm not asking." Hyles insisted.

"I couldn't agree more," Walters agreed. "Sergeant?"

"Hyles. Sergeant?"

"Walters. Twenty-Fourth Infantry, 'L' Company. Good to meet you, Sergeant Hyles. Your man's capable, but I agree with you: walking the streets alone is a bad idea."

"Perhaps we should take this inside?" Hyles suggested.

"I'll leave you to it," Walters said. "We're going to get some chow and hit the rack. It's been an exciting day. If you need us, we're around for a few more days before we head over to Dyea. You can find us camped just on the outskirts of town."

"You're bivouacked?" Hyles asked.

"The local establishments don't cater to us." Walters replied.

"What, soldiers?" Grant offered with a wry grin. "That seems to be going around in this town."

"Just so," Walters agreed.

"I won't keep you any longer. Again, thank you." Grant said and shook each of the soldier's hands in turn, ending with Sergeant Walters. "I owe you."

Stepping off the street and into the relative calm of the office, the buzz of the saloon's activity lingered in between Grant's ears. His hand brushed the doorframe as he entered, and his eyes scanned the room. The office was quiet, its sparse furniture offering no comfort against the growing sense of unease. On the far wall, a framed photograph of Queen Victoria hung slightly askew, as if even the Empire itself couldn't sit straight in this cooked town. Grant could not help but wonder what the next move would be, both for him and for Soapy.

Staff Sergeant Hyles returned to sit at his desk, kicked his boots up and leant back in his chair. Hands folded behind his head, he stared up at the ceiling with a look of quiet contemplation.

"What else happened out there, Grant?" he asked.

"I had a little chat with Soapy," Grant answered.

Jorge's eyebrows arched with concern, "How did that go?"

"Not as planned." Grant's mouth twitched into something between a smile and a grimace.

"You like sticking you head into the lion's mouth, hey?" Jorge scolded his friend. "That did nothing but ask for more trouble. Trouble none of us can afford." He turned to Hyles, looking for support, "Am I wrong?"

"Jorge's got a point," Hyles agreed. "Lion or no, Soapy's just been publicly embarrassed, by us. He doesn't need to be provoked any further. The thing is, with Soapy? He's never played fair, the only thing he respects is power. You didn't expect him to roll over, did you?"

"No," Grant replied. He took a moment and removed his Biltmore Stetson, tossing it onto the desk beside Hyles. "But I didn't expect him to be so damn, unflappable. He's got this town wrapped around his little finger."

Grant's mind churned as he thought back to the confrontation earlier. The way Soapy had leaned in, his smile like a predator's, mocking the Mountie for daring to challenge him. He had walked away, not beaten but certainly not victorious either. There had been no shooting, no blood spilled, but it had felt more dangerous than a dozen skirmishes.

"You're right about that," Hyles agreed. "He's even more unaffected with us, because we have no power here. We are out of country and without jurisdiction. We can protect ourselves but that's about it and he knows it. We are an annoyance. At best: an irritant. If he swats us like a fly, who's going to say anything?"

Jorge jumped in to add, "Soapy's entire network is well-armed and willing to do anything to protect his interests. He's got his fingers in everyone's pocket, from the saloons to the docks, to the Post Office. Even the local law, if you can call it that, are on his payroll."

Grant ran a hand through his hair, frustrated but trying to keep his composure. "That leaves us in a damn difficult position. There's no easy way out."

"Welcome to Skag," Hyles said, half-smiling. "This is the new and last North American frontier. Out here, everything's in flux. Chaos is the rule and order the exception. The moment we left the wharf, Soapy's grip on the town tightened yet again. You felt it. Today was just a warning."

Grant paced, running his hand along the edge of the table. "I underestimated him. I thought if we outmanoeuvred him on the wharf, we'd show him he couldn't control everything."

Hyles shook his head. "Soapy doesn't care about control. Not really. He cares about the illusion of control. If the town fears him, he wins."

Grant leaned against the wall, the reality of the situation settling in. He had hoped that a quick confrontation would be enough to scare Soapy off, but it was now clear that his reputation and influence were far greater than he had imagined.

"Is it too much to ask for a little bit of order?" Grant muttered. "Every time we try to make a move, it seems Soapy's ahead of us and waiting."

"Could be worse," Hyles said, tapping his fingers against the desk, his tone now more reflective. "At least you've made friends with the Army."

After a moment, Grant offered, "They're soldiers, not lawmen."

“True,” Hyles said. “However, that doesn’t mean we can’t use them to our advantage. When the time comes to move the mail, I’d suggest we ask them to escort us out of town. We can’t win by throwing punches or bullets; but, with the Army as our security, Soapy won’t risk getting on their bad side.”

Grant crossed the room and stood by the window, looking out across the street. The town had been buzzing with activity all day, but now, as the light began to fade into evening, the sounds had seemed to quieten. For a moment, everything seemed almost peaceful. Given his recent experiences in town, he knew better than to trust appearances.

“What are you thinking?” Hyles asked, his voice cutting through the silence.

Grant shook his head. “I don’t know yet. I thought we could handle this quickly. Take Soapy down, get the mail through, and restore some sense of order. But it’s not going to be that simple, is it?”

“No,” Hyles agreed, his voice thoughtful. “It’s never that simple. There’s a long road ahead of us, and we’ve got to be ready for whatever comes next.”

Grant turned from the window, his eyes meeting Hyles’ with a renewed determination. “What now?”

“We work your plan,” Hyles replied, standing up and walking to the map pinned to the wall. “We move the mail. Catch me up on what you’re thinking.”

Grant nodded, his mind already working through the challenges. His eyes flicked to the large map nailed to the wall on the left and sinister side of Queen Victoria’s portrait. He traced the winding lines of the trails over the mountain passes.

“Jorge and I were talking, and the toughest part of the journey are the Passes. White Pass is difficult terrain and the Chilkoot is a bottleneck.”

“The Chilkoot does have the reliability of the tramways,” Jorge observed. “The roads to the trams are good, the route is better than White Pass. It is reliable and, how you say: deliberate. The Chilkoot’s system can handle more regular traffic than the Dead Horse Trail.”

"Exactly," Grant replied. "Until the thaw reaches the upper passes, we still have the snow to navigate."

"We're also going to need to start thinking about the bigger picture," Hyles continued. "The railway over White Pass will change everything."

"Once it's built," Grant countered. "In the here and now? We still need horses and men on both sides of the border. It's going to be a logistical nightmare."

"Aye, and one helluva ride," Hyles muttered.

Jorge's tone was firm. "We can organize it."

"What have you figured out?" Grant asked.

"I have some reliable drivers who can navigate the route from Dyea to the Chilkoot. Most of them don't want anything to do with Soapy's racket. They just want to work and earn."

Grant leaned in, studying the map. "Do you trust them?"

Jorge nodded once. "As much as anyone can be trusted out here. We'll need the right people on the other side though."

"We have a relationship with one of the freighters there. They carried some, sensitive, cargo for us already." Grant replied, thinking back to bodies of his fallen brethren that the Orr and Tukey outfit had carried from Deep Lake back to Bennett. The loss of Young and Thompson seemed, in some ways, to have happened a long time ago, though the wound remained a fresh and ragged tear across Grant's heart and soul.

"Two teams," Hyles offered. "One for each trail. With alternate routes and staggered schedules that should make it impossible for Soapy to predict which load matters most."

"With Jorge working the Chilkoot and taking the bulk of the mail, I'll be the decoy crossing at White Pass. We can make it flashy and loud. He's most likely to chase that and me."

Jorge smiled slightly. "Risky. But clever."

"Everything out here's risky," Grant replied. "Have you found anyone to work the White Pass with me?"

"Si, there's a group of porters. They know the route better than anyone. They're Tlingit."

"Aye, I know them. They're tough," Hyles agreed. "White Pass and the Chilkoot have been trading routes for their people since; well, since before any of us were around messing the place up."

"Now that the Chilkoot is taken up by the tramways, they've been using White Pass more often." Jorge added.

"When can I meet them?" Grant asked.

"The head guy, George, he'll be here tomorrow," replied Hyles. "I've hired on a group of his family to work security on the warehouse. Speaking of which, how am I paying them?"

"Cash," Grant said, and retrieved the satchel Wood had given him from the bottom drawer of the desk next to the Sergeant.

"My favourite kind," laughed Jorge. "Shall we discuss my fee now?"

The night had grown heavy by the time Hyles and Grant stepped back out into the street. The air was colder now, threading its way under their coats. Jorge had left them earlier with his pockets filled with Wood's operating capital to address all the arrangements that still needed attention before morning.

As the two Mounties crossed into a narrower street, lamplight spilled out in golden strips through gaps in the clapboard buildings. Skagway was quiet in its own tense way, like a forest waiting for a storm. While whispers moved through town faster than footsteps, Grant noticed doors shutting and eyes peering at them through shuttered windows.

The raucous laughter of the saloons faded into hoarse murmurs. Skagway was never truly asleep, but this hour gave it the illusion of peace.

"I booked you a room at the Silver Antler," Hyles said, adjusting his wide-brimmed Stetson. "It's not much, but it's clean, and it doesn't ask too many questions. That's the best you can ask of a roof around here."

Grant nodded, following as Hyles led the way down a narrow boardwalk, the sound of their boots echoing in tandem. He hadn't realized how tired he was until now. Every muscle in his legs ached, and the tension in his shoulders, wound tight since the encounter with Soapy, was beginning to release in slow, painful increments.

"I never thought I'd see the day," Hyles muttered, "where Mounties would be walking through an American town like we were ghosts. Feared by some. Hated by others. But never seen as what we truly are."

Grant glanced sideways at him. "And what's that?"

"Men trying to keep the world from falling in on itself."

The Silver Antler sat at the far end of the street, its sign swaying lightly in the wind. The two-storey building had bay windows that flickered with lamplight. A tired woman at the desk handed them a key without speaking, her face drawn and hollow-eyed, as though she, too, had grown weary of the lawless rhythm of Skagway.

The room was small but serviceable. Wooden walls, a single bed, a washstand, and a narrow window overlooking the alley below. A small stove in the corner clicked softly as the embers inside it burned low.

Hyles lingered in the doorway. "You'll want to keep that Adams close to your beside. Soapy's men are brave when they think no one's watching."

"I'll be ready," Grant replied and patted the holster at his side.

"You always are," Hyles said, "I'll see you in the morning."

After Grant closed the door gently behind him, he stood for a moment in the stillness, listening to the wind rattling the windowpane. Then he sat on the edge of the bed and pulled off his boots. His Adams revolver lay on the nightstand, close enough to reach in the dark.

He didn't expect to sleep. But for now, he was warm, he was dry, and he was alive. Tomorrow, the fight would continue.

Later that night, after sleep refused to come, Grant sat alone at the desk by the window, writing in his field log by the light of a flickering oil lamp.

"The town remains in a fragile state. Soapy Smith's influence extends further than initially anticipated. Though we have removed the duties to safety, his control over Skagway continues to grow. Sergeant Hyles remains steadfast. The American Army, these Buffalo Soldiers, are proving to be brave, invaluable allies.

It's clear now this is more than a mission. It's a war of character, ours pitted against theirs. The post will get through. The law will hold. But at what cost, I wonder? We remain vigilant. Tomorrow, we begin again."

He closed the journal, its leather cover warm from his hand. Even now, the memory of Soapy's eyes, cold, calculating, and utterly unafraid, rattled something deep in his bones. It wasn't fear. No, it was something colder, something heavier: the realization that this wasn't over, not by a long shot.

Outside, the piano music had stopped. Only the wind remained, twisting through the town, its low whistle full of secrets.

CHAPTER XXII

Enter George

The warehouse on the Skagway wharf groaned with the weight of the months-long neglect. The stench of damp canvas, coal smoke, and mildew clung to every beam. Outside, the wind pressed in from the harbor, thick with the stench of low tide. Inside the warehouse there was silence. No laughter. No shouting. Just the shuffling of boots and the rustle of government mailbags long overdue for delivery.

Inside the purgatory of silence and canvas, Constable Grant crossed the warehouse floor with purpose. Since landing in Skagway, he'd been shot at, threatened, and outnumbered more times than he cared to count. However, nothing rattled him quite like the sight of this vast quantity of the mail. Piles of it. A siege of memory and bureaucracy. The letters bore postmarks from places as far off as London, Quebec, San Francisco. They bore names now lost to time. But each one had weight of emotion or necessity. Letters from wives to prospectors, payments from Ottawa, court summonses, payroll slips, pleas for news and requests to please come home.

Grant stood amid the dimness, letting the scent of mildew and old ink fill his lungs. The flicker of oil lamps threw his shadow across the bundled sacks. He rubbed his bruised and cracked knuckles and exhaled slowly.

Sergeant Hyles stood at a rough plank table near the back wall, a stub pencil ticking through a manifest. Jorge leaned over a crate nearby, adjusting the straps of a wooden sawbuck pack saddle. Retying the pack's cords, he was attaching canvas bags to its 'X' shaped frame with the precision of a surgeon. His face was calm, but Grant could see the tension in his shoulders. Every man in that room knew what they were stepping into.

"Hell of a thing," Jorge observed. "All of this mail. So many messages stuck here waiting."

"Waiting for their release. To fulfill their purpose," Grant continued the thought.

"Love letters, wedding news, final words from fathers to their sons. When the messages are delayed for so long, do you think they still matter?"

"They matter to me," Grant replied. "We need get them moving and over the mountains. That's my responsibility. I didn't think it before, but it weighs on me."

"You were supposed to pack light," Jorge quipped. "Not carry the weight of the world on your shoulders."

"The trail doesn't care about your letters," a voice called out from the warehouse's entryway.

Standing by the main entrance, still as a carved post and just as grounded, was a man Grant hadn't met before. He was short, broad across the shoulders, and wore his black hair in a tightly wrapped braid. His patched wool coat was layered over with hide and smoke-cured fabric. His moccasins were stained with salt and caked in town mud. His presence shifted the air. His eyes flicked to each motion in the room, Jorge's knots, Hyles' inventory, every step of Grant's pacing. The two security guards by the door nodded in silent salute to him as he entered.

"Gold, letters, they all weigh the same," the man said. "The trail only cares about your weakness."

Hyles looked up, and nodded toward the man, "You said you wanted someone who knew the trail. This is George."

No surname. None offered. None needed.

"Then we will carry no weakness," Grant offered in reply to the newcomer.

"No," George replied. "We all have weakness. But we will carry each other. The trail doesn't care who you are. Together, we are stronger."

Grant stepped forward, extending a hand, "Constable Stephen Grant."

George took the hand, his grip neither hard nor soft. His palm was calloused from years of labour, like bark stripped from an ancient tree. His eyes, dark and unreadable, scanned Grant's face like it was a landscape. Then he nodded once and released.

"You know the Dead Horse Trail well?" Grant asked.

George's reply came without hesitation. "I know what it has been and what it will ask of us."

For Grant, that was enough. He could see the wisdom and experience in George. He required no further words to believe in the man's mettle.

George walked past Grant to Jorge and looked over the canvas sacks stuffed with mail that he was rigging to the sawbucks.

"This load is uneven. You overpacked the left side. At the first incline, they'll strain. Lose a horse, you lose a day."

Jorge looked at what George was pointing to, his eyes narrowing. Then he nodded, "I didn't catch that."

George adjusted a cinch by an inch and stepped back. "The trail will catch everything." He continued to examine the other sawbucks that Jorge had packed.

"Have you had any dealings with Soapy Smith?" Grant asked.

George didn't answer immediately as he tied a knot, tested it, then straightened. His face didn't change, but something colder passed through his eyes.

"Once," he said.

Grant waited. The silence stretched.

"He offered me work," George said. "Said he needed a packer who didn't ask questions. Eastbound job. Light load. High pay."

"What was it?"

George's mouth twitched, it was not quite a smile.

"Didn't ask. Didn't carry it, either."

Grant watched him carefully. "How'd he take to that?"

George met his eye, "Someone followed me a day later. Followed me all day. Then he came into my camp at night to change my mind. He threatened my family."

Grant raised a brow. "And?"

George looked back down at the next sawbuck and pulled on a cinch strap. His voice stayed even, when he said, "He doesn't shake hands anymore."

The cold silence that followed said more than any threat could. Grant gave a slow nod as George stepped past him. “Smith thinks he owns the trail. He doesn’t. The trail has its own rules. It doesn’t forgive and neither do I.”

Hyles gave a short, bitter laugh. “George, I do love the way you talk. Speaking of Mr. Smith, two of his goons were at the docks during the night, asking after you, Grant. One had your name written on a card.”

“Still breathing,” Grant replied. “Still a target.”

“They won’t stop until someone collects that bounty,” Hyles added. He closed the ledger and leaned forward, tapping the map spread out on the table. “It will only end once you’re dead or Smith’s dead. For now, they know we’re up to something. They don’t know what. Yet.”

Grant, George and Jorge joined Hyles around the table and looked down at the map.

“They will,” said Jorge. “As soon as we load the horses.”

“Smith joked about us being postmen. He knows enough. He’s clever,” Grant said. “He’s not just any thug.”

“No,” Hyles disagreed. “He’s a thug, one with a good tailor.”

“He does have a new hat,” Jorge added. “Quite nice, actually.”

The group laughed, and the tension in the room broke for a moment. The laughter had cracked the tension, but it did not dispel it. The unspoken truth lingered underneath that one wrong turn or mistake could spell disaster for their entire plan.

Grant rubbed his thumb along the edge of the map as he stared again at the red lines of their routes crossing the page like blood filled veins. Every choice he made would carve a new path through danger. Jorge would go one way, he and George another. Only his name was marked for death, but every man who followed him shared in that bounty’s risk. He had a make peace with sending them all out into the dark without any guarantee of success. He had his orders and that had to be enough.

“Thoughts?” Grant asked the group.

George traced his finger along the route from Skagway towards White Pass. “Here,” he said, tapping a section. “Rockfall last week. The trail changed. We follow the ridgeline north. Mudslide risk here, and here. We cross upstream. Safer footing.”

"Noted," Grant said. "You'll call the line."

George nodded once.

"Tomorrow's the day. Sergeant Walters and his men will meet us here in the morning to escort us out of town."

"These soldiers will stay with us?" George asked.

"Yes," Grant answered. They'll escort us to the border."

George nodded his head and said no more.

"After we make our way through town, making a scene as we go," Grant continued, "that's when Jorge will load the rest of the post into the boats and ferry it across to Dyea."

"Si, I cannot wait," Jorge replied. "Get me out of this room, papa!"

The group fell back into a tense silence. Outside, a distant boom echoed from the rail yard on the outskirts of town, more dynamite clearing the way for the White Pass and Yukon Route. The railway was coming, sure as the tide, but not fast enough to help them now. Tomorrow, they would be more than men with mailbags. They would be a thread pulled tight between civilization and the wilderness. A thread that could snap at any moment. But not yet. The mail would move. And with it, the future.

CHAPTER XXIII

Taking the Mail

Dawn crept into Skagway like a nervous intruder, its light was pale and reluctant under the tin-coloured overcast sky. The morning's light touched the tops of the pine-stubbled ridges, long before it would filter down into the shadowed streets of the town. Spring fog hung thick along the wharf, its trailing tendrils slithering up alleyways and around crooked shacks, muffling the usual sounds of morning. A dull chill clung to everything, wetting wood, canvas, and skin. A steam whistle moaned, long and low, from the half-finished rail yard, a mournful call that echoed off the mountains and back into town like a ghost unsure of its path.

As the postal convoy began to assemble out front of the warehouse, there was no fanfare. No ceremonial send-off. No cheering crowd. Just the dull thud of boots and hooves on planks, punctuated by the quiet grunt of horses being loaded down under the harnesses of their sawbuck pack saddles.

Constable Grant stood at the mouth of the warehouse, adjusted the strap on his rifle and pulled his coat tight across his chest. His fingers were stiff. Everything was damp. The sleeves of his uniform, the leather of his gloves, the breeches stuffed into his high riding boots.

He watched as George inspected their final loadout. The Tlingit guide was adjusting the cinches on the lead packhorse. Steam rose from the animal's nostrils, its flanks twitching beneath the weight of the mail sacks. Finished, he whispered something in the animal's ear and patted its neck in reassurance before he turned and barked out a set of orders in his clipped Tlingit dialect. His team of four other packers acknowledged him with quiet nods and gestures. They had worked with an efficient silence through the morning, moving the sacks of mail sealed in canvas and tarred leather onto the backs of the waiting horses. The animals had snorted clouds into the cold morning, stamping impatiently on the wharf.

This was it. The first official mail run over the Dead Horse Trail. Dangerous. Necessary. And it was his to lead. Jorge stood nearby, his arms crossed and face solemn in the dawn haze. He wouldn't be going with them. His load would follow the Chilkoot Trail, and he would wait to see if Soapy took the bait and followed Grant's progress over the mountains before he left by boat for Dyea.

"You're taking the hard road," Jorge observed quietly.

"I know," Grant replied.

Jorge looked out at the fog. "The hard road suits you."

They shook hands and without another word Jorge turned and disappeared back into the warehouse.

Sergeant Hyles approached next, offering Grant a folded map in his outstretched hand.

"I spotted Tom Blanchard and Denny Crawley waiting at the end of the wharf. They work for Soapy. They're watching and waiting. No reason for them to be out here except looking for trouble. You'll want to watch your flanks."

Grant nodded, took the map and slid it into the inner folds of his uniform jacket and rebuttoned the red serge closed. "I appreciate it, Staff Sergeant."

"He's not going to let this go, you know?"

"I don't expect him to. I just want him to focus on me so Jorge can slip through."

Hyles hesitated, then said, "Make sure you come back. We've got plenty of work to do here."

Grant gave a brief, grim smile. "That's the plan."

"You stay safe, Constable," he said and offered his hand.

Grant gripped the Sergeant's hand firmly. "The mail comes first, but I'll deliver myself safe and sound too."

A simple nod passed between them. Then Hyles stepped back from the convoy.

The rest of the convoy was ready. Four Buffalo Soldiers, led by Sergeant Walters, stood by with their rifles slung and eyes sharp.

They had volunteered for the escort. Their uniforms were clean, their boots well-worn. These were proven men who knew how to move in silent efficiency.

Grant looked once more at the assembled line: eight pack horses, sixty sacks, ten men and a guide. It was a thin line between two worlds. Between order and wilderness.

"Let's move," he said to George.

George clicked his tongue, brought the horses to order and they left the wharf in silence. As the convoy made their turn off the planks and onto the muddy streets, Grant spied the lookouts that Hyles had warned him about. The two figures were lingering near the edge of a shuttered supply shack across the street. One leaned against the wall, a battered derby pulled low over his brow; the other shifted from foot to foot, glancing nervously between the convoy and the road ahead.

Grant met the eyes of the shorter one: a pale, rat-faced man with greasy hair and a twitch in his left cheek. Recognition flared in the man's eyes, and then he turned, whispered something to his companion, and darted off down an alley at a jog.

"Runner," George murmured, almost to himself.

Grant's jaw tightened. "He's going to tell Smith."

No one needed to say more. The convoy kept moving. But the silence now felt different, tighter. Watched. The other goon, wearing the derby, trailed the convoy at a comfortable, but noticeable distance behind Walters and the other soldiers.

As they travelled along Broadway Street, mud sucked at the horses' hooves. Faces appeared behind dusty windows, behind the warped glass of saloons and general stores. Lopsided buildings barely held together with hammered nails and hope. Faces watched from behind curtain cracks and saloon windows. Despite the early hour, civilians, barkeeps, barmaids, gamblers, miners, all stood frozen and watched as if the convoy were a funeral procession. No one waved. No one spoke. Children peered up from behind their mothers' skirts. A few men leaned against posts, chewing tobacco as they watched with a detached interest. The town had the look of a place waiting to see which way the wind would blow and if shots would be fired in the coming minutes of the group's passage.

A young woman stood by the roadside holding a child on her hip. She didn't wave, didn't speak. Just watched, lips tight, eyes tracking the mail bags like they carried her future.

"Let's be sure to let them know we're leaving, George." Grant said to his guide. "We'll turn down Sixth, if you please."

George nodded his head, without anything further to add.

When the convoy turned left off Broadway and onto 6th Avenue the wind shifted. Ahead of them, sat the squat, narrow whitewashed building that was Jeff Smith's Parlor. Gathered outside was a crowd of men, some waiting for entry, some to see what was coming, and the rest, armed men in Soapy Smith's employ. Approaching the crowd, the voice Grant was hoping to hear rang out.

"Constable!"

It carried across the street, clear and dry as a crack of gunfire. Grant turned in his saddle towards the gathered crowd.

There he stood, Jefferson Randolph "Soapy" Smith, on the front stoop of the Parlor, dressed like a banker at Sunday brunch. A long, dark overcoat hung open to reveal a crisp waistcoat, gold watch chain and polished boots. The new hat Jorge had complimented sat square atop his oiled hair. No revolver at his waist, no visible threat. Just a silver-headed cane in his gloved right hand and a knowing smile on his lips.

"Where you planning on leaving without saying goodbye?" Smith called out, his tone smooth and mocking. "Headed somewhere important this morning?"

Grant veered a few steps towards him, stopping his mount at the edge of the muddy street. "Mail run," he said flatly. "First of many."

Soapy whistled low and looked at the convoy as it continued to proceed past. "That's a fine-looking collection of mail sacks you've got there. Heavy, too. Wonder what's inside? Hope it's not more tax forms."

"That's not for me to know. We respect things like order, decency, a person's privacy. The little things that everyone should get to enjoy."

Soapy's smile widened, "I thought that was whiskey and women?"

Sergeant Walters and the Buffalo Soldiers were bringing up the rear of the column. As they drew closer to the Parlor, Soapy gave them a cursory glance and said, “Still keeping questionable company, I see. You Mounties and your grand illusions. Out there,” he waved lazily toward the looming mountains, “there’s no uniform that can save you. No courtrooms. No comforts. Just snow, blood and a long way to fall.”

Grant didn’t take the bait. He was close enough to see the tightness in Soapy’s eyes. The man was calm, but only just. Behind that polished grin was fury, and Grant could see it. Feel it.

“You enjoy your morning,” Grant said, turning his horse back toward the caravan. He paused to adjust his gloves slowly, just enough to stall a few more seconds.

“You’ve got a whole town on a string, Smith. But that string won’t hold forever.”

Soapy’s smile thinned, but he didn’t step down from the Parlor’s stoop.

“Every town’s just a stage, Constable. You know that. Lights come up, you take your part. When the act’s over, nobody remembers who was honest. Just who made it out alive.”

Grant’s voice stayed calm. “That’s where we differ. I’d rather be forgotten doing the right thing than remembered for stealing the show.”

Soapy nodded, almost like he respected the line. “Then I guess you’ll die with your boots on and a moral in your mouth. Shame. I always liked your style.”

“And I never liked yours.”

“Ah, but you never looked away. That’s what makes us kin, in some crooked way. You and me, we both know this place won’t be tamed with law books.”

“No,” Grant said. “But we’ll try anyway.”

Smith's expression turned thoughtful for a breath. Then he tapped his silver-headed cane twice on the porch boards, “Don’t forget to write.”

“I’ll send you a postcard from the Klondike,” Grant called out over his shoulder.

With that, Smith stepped back into the shadows of the Parlor, the heavy door closing behind him with a thud that echoed down the street.

From the corner of his eye, Grant saw the rat-faced man from the wharf reappear near the side of a bakery. He had been joined by two more rough-looking figures. They didn't follow close, not yet, but they lingered, like the smoke from a wet fire that refuses to disperse. They stayed in rifle range, just close enough to remind Grant he was being watched.

As the convoy passed the last stretch of town, the world began to shift. The buildings gave way to supply yards and rough roadbeds. Piles of lumber and crates were stacked high beside their path. After the buildings had thinned and fallen away, the shadows of Soapy's men continued to trail them, demonstrating that his influence was not confined to the limits of town.

Grant looked back, past his three stalkers, out towards the harbour. From their vantage point, he could see the trio of tugs they had hired to carry the rest of the post across the inlet to Dyea. They had pulled away from the far side of the wharves and were underway. He could barely make out the figures on their decks. He imagined that one of them was Jorge standing on the lead tug's stern, watching the town drop away as they steamed across the water. Two routes. One mission. He sighed a breath of relief, wished his friend well and said a silent prayer for their safety.

George, watching the same scene, gave a short nod. "He'll make Dyea and be on the trail by nightfall. If the weather holds."

"Let's hope so. For all our sakes," Grant replied as he clenched his gloved hand tighter around the reins and looked ahead.

After crossing the Skagway River, they continued to follow the road leading them towards the foothills. It skirted the burgeoning railway's construction. It was a chaotic melee of smoke, timber, and labour. The full scale of the railway's advance became more pronounced. These were the active front lines of a brutal campaign, not the neat order of Skagway's nearly finished rail yard. It was an ongoing battle for conquest over the topography. The steel spine of the White Pass & Yukon Route was carving its way northward, a brutal scar lengthening itself into the wilderness.

Closest to town, they found the polished precision of the tracklayers. Steel rails were being guided into place by crane and cart, laid atop fresh-cut ties and hammered down by crews in blackened gloves and ash-caked shirts. Others hauled thick iron rails off timber carts in anticipation of their placement next along the steel artery being laid down. The road here narrowed, and George led the horses single file past a line of fresh iron rails waiting to be laid.

The steam crane groaned as it hoisted another section of track, its cables trembling under strain. Below it, the gang with sledges moved and swung in a sustained iron rhythm: four strokes, shift, four more. The Chinese labourers worked in fast, silent teams, their hammers ringing as they drove in spikes with a method nearing the mechanical. Their work sang out like hammering war drums. Dust hung thick in the morning air, as foremen barked commands in English, punctuated by curses. Standing atop wooden trestles, their voices were hoarse and urgent. Mule carts rattled by with more iron and timber. Smoke from pine pitch fires drifted over the site, used to keep blackflies at bay and boil sap for sealing timber. Here and there, sweat-drenched men paused only to swallow bitter coffee or catch their breath before returning to the line.

The further they travelled from Skagway, the more primitive and desperate the work became. Next came the graders, the earthmovers, toiling in low ditches hastily cut into a land that refused to cooperate. Their boots sank into churned clay as they swung picks and shovels to level out the track's future path. Backs bent, shirts soaked through with effort as stones were cleared, soil was packed and more trenches were cut. A chain of men passed baskets of gravel, pausing only when water barrels arrived.

Past them, stump gangs strained against pine-rooted obstacles. Teams of workers, wrapped in oilskin and flannel, shouted above the clatter of chains and iron. A row of oxen groaned against the strain of a crude stump-puller, uprooting ancient pine trunks. Sawyers followed, working in pairs with long crosscut saws, teeth screaming through sap-soaked trunks slicing them into workable pieces, while others cleared brush with long-handled axes to clear the grading route.

Beyond that, the black powder crews were a separate beast. Gaunt, smoke-blackened men worked with eerie calm, drilled holes into granite and hammered in charges. A foreman with a whistle paced along the line, counting down, then calling clear. A moment's silence and then came the thunder. The earth shuddered, and showers of debris rained down. Grant thought back to Lillian and her dynamite blasting skills as the convoy's horses skittered, ears flicking after the last round of blasts that had rolled through the basin like rippling cannon fire.

Further still along the trail, they reached the cutting crews. Cant hooks clacked as teams rolled felled logs away from the cut. The workers here were filthier, slower, their muscles twitching from exhaustion. One man collapsed onto his knees, coughing into a rag. No one stopped to help.

Swinging axes in endless arcs, the timbermen ahead were clearing the once untouched fingers of the forest. The air was filled with the smell of pine resin and sweat and woodsmoke. Here, the line had not yet been drawn, only imagined. Trees fell with deep groans, their trunks crashing into the underbrush as shouted warnings echoed across the valley. Men who looked like they hadn't seen sleep in days, their faces hollow-eyed, their hands blistered raw. Grant nodded to a group of them as they passed. One man gave a slow wave with two fingers still wrapped in torn cloth. The others just stared. Red jacketed lawmen weren't a common sight out here, especially ones headed in the wrong direction, escorted by soldiers, away from town, into the wild.

The convoy had moved alongside this living corridor of ambition and fatigue, passing the disciplined chaotic siege engine of order to the realm beyond. The wild, where no sounds remained but hooves on the trail and the creaking of pack saddles as their horses' breath flared up in the mist. The road climbed gradually, drawing them toward the foot of the mountains. Pine needles lay wet on the path, and the smell of snowmelt and thawed soil filled the air. They had returned to pristine sanctuary of natural order and Grant felt like he could breathe, unencumbered, once again.

Skagway was already beginning to feel like memory.

"Trail proper starts beyond that ridge," George said, pointing with his chin.

Grant followed his gaze. The path cut along a rocky shelf, then disappeared into a dense wall of trees.

"Your friends are still following us," George observed.

Grant felt a familiar knot tighten in his gut. He turned in the saddle and looked back once more. The valley below was misty now. Smoke curled from chimneys in town. The rails gleamed faintly like threads trying to stitch the town to something bigger.

"We'll see who makes it through," Grant muttered.

And so, they rode on.

CHAPTER XXIV

The Perils of the Trail

The trail rose ahead in a long incline climbing the slippery slate cliffs of what had become known as Devil's Hill. It had been churned by the hooves of pack animals and scarred by the remains of those that had failed the climb. A single misstep by any of them could lead to a five-hundred-foot fall to their doom. The stench of death lay faint in the air, old and weather-worn, but persistent. The Dead Horse Trail had only begun but by this point, it had already earned its name a hundred times over. Named not in jest, but for the literal thousands of animals that had died trying to scale its shifting cliffs, ice-choked gullies, and bottomless bogs.

Grant rode near the front of the convoy, rifle across his lap, close behind George, whose quiet manner masked a lifetime of trail knowledge. As the Tlingit Guide scanned the tree line, the Buffalo Soldiers brought up the rear in silence. Like George, their eyes were never still for long.

The fog that had settled in since reaching the foothills had refused to lift. Pooling in the gullies and swirling across the trail, its uncomfortable caress pressed against their skin like damp wool. They had travelled a good hour beyond the last sign of the rail crews when George raised a hand. The caravan halted behind him, the only sound the snort of horses and the shifting of boots and hooves.

Grant eased his horse forward. "What is it?"

George said nothing, just pointed ahead with his chin. Above them, on a bluff, stood a lone figure. Still and watching them, like a statue of warning which had been carved into the ridge itself.

“Rifle,” Private Baker could be heard to mutter from the rear.

The figure didn’t move. Didn’t speak. After a few moments, they just faded backwards into the mist.

Grant felt the frustration growing in his chest. They had been shadowed for too long. First through Skagway, then the construction zone, and now, here in the wilderness, a new group was making itself known. Soapy’s men weren’t subtle, and they weren’t giving up. He could feel it in his bones. The convoy was being hunted slowly, not to steal the mail, but to unravel them and eventually claim Grant’s head as the ultimate prize.

They pressed on.

By midafternoon, the trail narrowed to a barely passable channel between high rock walls and the ten-foot-tall boulders that scattered the ascent up Porcupine Hill. Mud-slick and treacherous, one of the horses slipped, kicked hard, panicked, but George calmed it before it could tumble. The packers checked the cinches and reins, working together quickly and without sharing a word. The shared knowledge was apparent to Grant as he observed their work and manner.

As they climbed, the smell of rot grew stronger. There were carcasses of horses lining the trail, the ribs of some yellowing in the thaw. Turkey Vultures circled high above waiting for the chance to descend and scavenge without interruption of the trail’s traffic. Even the soldiers, stoic as they were, began to show signs of wear. Each step was a reminder: this land didn’t care who you were. Mountie or outlaw. Civilized or savage. Soldier or local. The trail took what it wanted and at a time of its choosing.

That night, camp was made beneath a copse of bent pines overlooking a gully. The fire crackled low, barely enough to warm their boots. George and the other packers worked silently, tending the horses that had shed their heavy packs of mail. Sergeant Walters ladled beans and smoked bacon into tin bowls while his men sat in silence, eyes fixed on the trees. Grant stood just beyond the glow of the campfire, his eyes also scanning shadows cast across the trees.

“We’re being tracked,” said Private Hill.

“We’ve been followed since Skagway,” Grant replied. “They’re not closing in, but this new group up ahead worries me.”

"They're waiting for something," muttered Private Baker.

"They're waiting for the trail to act against us," George said. "The new ones have been waiting for this. They must be staying up at White Pass City."

Sergeant Walters set down the tin pot with a clank, "They want to box us in."

There was a long silence before Grant returned to the fire. "I'm done waiting. If they want to trail us like wolves, let's give them something to choke on. Tomorrow, I suggest we end this."

"How?" asked Walters.

Grant looked to George. "You know this terrain. Is there a place for us to stop and draw both groups in?"

George nodded once. "I know where the trail bends and narrows. There's a switchback shelf there with a choke point. The trees are thick on one side and a drop off on the other. If we get there first, we control it. We hold there and wait for them to come to us."

"Hell yeah," Private Hill said and spat into the dirt. "This feels like some good trouble."

Grant looked to the others. "We give them a choice: leave... or bleed. Agreed?"

Solemn faces, wreathed in the firelight, nodded in silent assent. Sergeant Walters passed Grant a tin plate, steaming with beans, and asked, "Still want to send that postcard?"

They broke camp before dawn. The fire was out, coals buried, the scent of burnt coffee clinging to their gloves. Every man moved with sharpened silence, the kind that followed a night of uneasy rest. The windless air was broken only by the groan of saddles and the occasional cough. Cold light gathered in the east, but it barely reached them through the thick canopy's haze.

As his breath misted in the dark, Grant moved with grim purpose. Checking each pack strap, he nodded to the soldiers one by one as they climbed towards the place George said would be to their advantage.

George gathered his two chosen packers, men quiet as shadows, and led them north into the trees. They didn't speak. They just vanished.

The rest of the column moved along the designated route.

After a few hours of climbing, the trail ahead of them curved sharply into a rocky saddle, narrowing into a cruel strip of land that clung to the edge of the mountain. On the left, was a steep drop into shale and pine scrub. On the right were dense woods hunched tight against the rock walls, bristling with spruce and silent possibility. It was the kind of place where an ambush felt inevitable; or, perfect. It all was all dependent on which side was on the receiving end of the surprise.

Grant led the convoy off the trail and behind a jagged outcrop. Cloaked in the low branches and thick scrub, from here they had elevation and concealment. Most important was some space for the pack train away from what could become a deadly gunfight. Each man took up their position among boulders and tree stumps. Rifles rested across their knees, while breaths were held tight in their chests.

Time passed. A hawk circled above. A gust stirred the branches of the nearby spruce and pine. No footfalls. No voices. Just the cold stillness and uncertainty of waiting.

Every man in the ambush line had their own rhythm for silence. Some stared down their rifle sights. Others closed their eyes, listening for the small noises along the trail that betrayed someone was coming. Grant kept his gaze fixed on the bend, knuckles white on his rifle's grip. The trail remained empty.

Then, there was movement.

The first group of their stalkers stepped into view as they ventured around the bend just below the convoy's concealed positions. Hunched over and trudging along, steam rose around their collars thanks to the exertion of the climb. One was the rat-faced man from Skagway. The other two were broader, but the climb had rendered them far reduced from their capabilities in-town, at sea level. One was red-bearded, with a rifle slung casually across his shoulder. The other: dark haired, with a terribly scarred face from acne or a likely worse cause. Their pace was slow, arrogant. They weren't expecting resistance or any real challenge.

Grant lifted his hand, signalling the others to make ready.

Soapy's men approached the narrowest section of the switchback, where the drop to the left yawned out over the brambles and loose shale to a hundred-foot drop through the air to a very certain death.

Grant stepped out first, his rifle raised and challenged them, "Drop your rifles."

The men froze. The red-bearded one went for his weapon, only too slow. Walters fired from above, the shot cracking like a slap of steel against stone. The round smacked into the dirt inches from the man's boots, kicking up slush and pebbles.

After he stepped into the open to join Grant, Walters said calmly, "The next one goes through your chest."

Soapy's stalkers remained frozen, their eyes wide. The cord of tension had been drawn tight as a hangman's noose. Just who would become the condemned was the question being briefly contemplated by both sides.

"You're a long way from town," Grant said. "This is the last time you follow us. I'm giving you the opportunity to turn around now. Or, you can stay and find out what dying on the Dead Horse Trail feels like."

The red-bearded man shifted, "You gonna kill us for walking a trail, Copper?"

"No," Grant said. "But I'm Stephen Grant and for hunting me, I'll bury you." To punctuate his point, he cocked the hammer on his Winchester.

Before they could respond, there was a rustle from the upper slope. Another five men appeared, descending the trail. The advance group had their rifles raised not in readiness, but in confusion. They had expected to find and harass their quarry much earlier in the day. George stepped out behind them, silent and steady, his weapon already drawn. The packers flanked him on either side, their rifles trained and ready to fire.

"Easy," George said, voice cold as the snow. "I never miss."

The trap was complete. All of Soapy's men were caught in the chokepoint. They had little choice but to comply with what they were being asked or die for their troubles.

Grant advanced slowly. "You've got a choice," he said, eyes sweeping across them. "Strip your weapons. Toss your boots. Walk back to Skagway. If we see you again, we won't have this conversation twice."

The rat-faced man snarled, “You expect us to crawl back barefoot?”

“That’s the mercy,” Grant said. “The alternative’s worse.”

The red-bearded one looked across the drop behind them. Then at Walters, then towards George. He saw no room for defiance.

No one moved. For a heartbeat, it seemed like it might erupt with someone twitching toward a bad end; but that moment never came. They chose capitulation. They were bullies, used to having the upper hand but they chose instead to live and run another day. One by one, they gave in. Rifles were dropped. Knives tossed. Boots yanked off and flung to the ground in disgust.

Grant nodded to George. “Have a couple of your men trail them out. If they veer off their return to Skag, shoot one. Let the others watch.”

George gestured, and two of his packers moved in. Silent and efficient, they herded the barefoot men back down the trail. As they vanquished left their shame was more visible than their fear.

Only when the last of their shadows were lost in the trees did Grant lower his rifle.

“Think they’ll talk?” Hill asked.

“They’ll talk,” Grant said. “Anyone thinking about following in their footsteps is going to consider that proposition twice.”

The air felt different to Grant now. Not safe, never that, but cleaner. Sharper. Clearer. The post would get through. The Klondike depended on it. And for once, they were no longer the hunted. They were the warning on the trail. They had become the wolves, and they had sent the sheep back to town.

CHAPTER XXV

Full Circle

The sky was a bruised slate grey when the convoy crested the last ridge before the White Pass summit. Snow fell in fine, angled lines, blown sideways by the winds that never quite stopped howling in this high country. It knifed across the exposed rock, dragging flurries across the switchbacks like tattered ghosts. The horses were breathing hard, their flanks quivering beneath layers of frost and sweat, their breath rising in thick, ragged plumes. The men looked no better. Their coats were stiff with ice, brows crusted with snowmelt, faces hollowed by the exertion of their march.

Ahead, nestled below the looming rise of mountain's peaks, was the border outpost. The huddle of crude timber structures and tents sagging under snow-weight were scattered around the Log Cabin itself. Smoke curled up from chimneys and stove pipes to be caught and dispersed in the winds. Sleds and crates lay half-buried in the snowbanks on either side of the groove the continual traffic's passing had worn through the outpost itself. It looked more to Grant like a besieged winter camp than a border station. Having made the climb from the coast, Grant had himself become a Stampeder. He now held a new appreciation and insight into what it meant to arrive at the border from the Alaskan side. He could see his fellow Mounties at work around the site, and above it all, like a promise carved into the cold, flew the bright lines of the Union Jack from its weather-beaten pole. The standard's faded colours snapped in the wind against the frozen backdrop of white.

Grant reined in his mount and sat still in the saddle for a long moment as he stared at the border station. His breath clouded in front of him, fading into the wind. Around him, the convoy was gathered in quiet triumph. George stood beside the lead horse, hand resting on its mane, eyes scanning the camp. The other Tlingit packers soothed the exhausted horses that were eager to shed the loads they had brought this far. The two who had escorted the outlaws Grant had relieved of their boots back down to Skagway had caught back up with them within a few days and had not appeared any the wearier for the additional travel. Sergeant Walters and his Buffalo Soldiers drew up behind, their blue woollen coats crusted in frost, their rifles slung, and shoulders squared.

They had made the border. All of them.

Every sack of mail was intact. Every soul was still standing. Grant cast a hope and a prayer out onto the wind that Jorge and his group were experiencing similar success.

The distant sound of a bell rang out twice. It brought Grant's attention back to the present moment. The sentries on watch had seen the convoy and rang the bell to alert the post of the group's approach.

"Push on George. Let's get across," Grant urged his guide.

Frost clung to the horses' fetlocks and their breath steamed like engines as George led them on single file into the summit camp. They obeyed George's steady hand, and the entire convoy, cold and spent, found a rhythm in the familiar aches generated by the last mile's climb.

The crossing of the border was marked by nothing more than a hand-hewn sign and a pair of crossed poles nailed to pine trunks. To Grant, it felt like a gateway, a threshold. At the very least, it was a personal achievement to return to after his mission.

At the camp's centre, the brooding menace of the Maxim gun sat mounted on a reinforced sled between sandbagged crates, its barrel dusted with snow. Manned by a Constable with a scarf wrapped tight over his face, its presence said everything about the uncertainty of the borderlands, and how close civilization still sat to the edge of chaos.

Flanked by two constables and a civilian surveyor with a map case slung over one shoulder, Inspector Strickland stood waiting as the convoy crossed the invisible line in the Dominion of Canada. The collar of Strickland's Buffalo coat was turned up against the wind, his fur hat pulled low over his brow as though he'd been standing there for hours. His boots were braced wide in the snow, a small puff of frost escaped his nose as he exhaled over the ice crusted across his moustache. Scanning each face of the new arrivals, he gave them a short nod in greeting.

"Constable Grant. I see you've brought the post."

"Hello Inspector. We're only the first wave," Grant said.

"The first of many, of that I have no doubt." Strickland replied and looked past him at the team: the silent packers, the imposing George, the baggage-laden horses and the disciplined Buffalo Soldiers,

His gaze lingered on the Americans, his brow tightening. "I take it these men are with you?"

"Yes, sir." Grant answered. "Sergeant Walters and his men are United States Army, 'L' Company, twenty-fourth Infantry. Volunteered to help us see the mail safely through."

Strickland's mouth twitched, but it was not quite a grimace. "An unusual escort for Her Majesty's mail."

"Soapy Smith made things more complicated. Without them, we'd be down more than just Constables Thompson and Young."

Strickland studied Walters a long moment, then stepped forward and offered a gloved hand. "Sergeant Walters, I am Inspector Strickland. On behalf of the North-West Mounted Police, welcome to Canada and thank you for your service."

Walters shook his hand firmly. "Glad to have helped. We all wore frost for the same cause."

Strickland gave a brief nod and turned back to Grant. "Come inside. Warm up. We've much to talk about."

Inside the Log Cabin itself, the warmth hit Grant like a wall. A stove glowed in the corner of the main room, its iron belly alive with fire. He gratefully stripped off his Buffalo coat, stomped his boots, and wrapped his fingers around a blisteringly hot tin mug to thaw them out one painful digit at a time. The scorching black tea in the mug was so strong it could have stripped paint. Grant drank it down deeply and greedily.

Strickland sat across from him at his small desk and opened a logbook before him. The oil lamp between them cast long shadows across the rough wooden walls. As Grant's gloves sat drying on the stove's rail, steam curled from their seams. "I want a full report," Strickland said, his tone clipped but not unkind.

Grant leaned forward, cradling the mug of tea. He recounted everything, starting with his plan with Jorge; the ambush in Deep Lake that had claimed Constables Thompson and Young; the desperate defence on the docks in Skagway; and, the long, punishing crawl up and over the Dead Horse Trail. He detailed the attempted assassinations and the later shadowing of the convoy by Soapy's men, the ambush they had staged in return, and the condition of the mail when it finally crossed the border, along with the potential progress of Jorge's team crossing the Chilkoot.

His voice never wavered, but Strickland could hear the weight behind each word. The kind of weight that didn't just vanish with rest and simple reflection.

Strickland scratched notes in the margins of the logbook, pausing only once to refill Grant's mug from a battered kettle. He asked some precise questions and jotted down the answers with the efficiency of a man used to reporting chaos in summary form.

When it was done, Strickland closed the book and sat back, regarding Grant for a long moment.

"You've done well, You did your duty," he said. "More than that: you got Wood and the duties out. You brought the mail, and you brought the men following you through safely. Despite losing Thompson and Young, that counts as a win. Several wins, in fact. You should be proud."

"Hard to see anything objectively at present, Inspector."

"Of course," Strickland replied, as he glanced toward the stove. "I'll write to Steele. I suspect he'll be both impressed and furious. He tends to be that way when someone either disobeys direct orders or pulls off the impossible."

Grant managed a tired smile, "The job's not done yet."

"True enough," Strickland agree, then asked, "What of Smith?"

"Still in Skagway. Watching. Waiting. We gave him a warning. I don't expect he'll heed it. Men like Soapy don't walk away. Not until someone makes them."

Strickland nodded slowly, running a gloved thumb along the edge of the logbook. "His time will come."

Grant sipped his tea. "He's holding onto Skagway like it's his last card. He's got the town so tight in his grip they don't know who's robbing them worse: him, or the trail."

"He's a rotten beam in the woodwork. Dangerous, clever enough to know when to step aside, only too proud to ever do it."

"There's no local law to push back. The army will be kept at a distance, they'll be camped near Dyea: out of sight and out of mind. Civil authorities have no real hold. It's a rigged game down there. It'll take the people itself for anything to change."

Strickland's gaze hardened. "What did you make of him?"

Grant didn't answer immediately. He looked toward the window where snow drifted against the frame. "He's unflappable. He's not scared of anything, I think. At least, that's how he projects himself to the outside world. I almost respect him for that alone. Otherwise, he's insufferable. An arrogant criminal"

A Constable who Grant did not recognize leaned inside the cabin's entrance. He said to Strickland, "Dinner's ready, sir. They've made room in the barracks to hold a mess for the whole team."

Strickland stood. "Come on, Grant. Let's eat."

The evening's celebratory mess had been hastily set up inside the rough wooden barracks, a drafty but welcome shelter from the cold. The long, narrow room was packed to the walls, with plank benches crowded tight around tables fashioned from old shipping crates and salvaged boards. Lanterns burned low, their warm lights pooling in amber circles that flickered against the frost-laced windows.

It was tight, loud, and it smelled of smoke, boiled meat, and wet wool. But it was warm, and it was enough.

The Buffalo Soldiers claimed a corner near the stove, their laughter rising and falling in tired rhythms. Private Hill and Private Baker jostled elbows over a second helping of stew while

Sergeant Walters sat at the end, his posture relaxed but his eyes always watchful.

The Tlingit packers sat together near the far wall, speaking little, but their quiet pride was evident in their posture and eyes. George sat apart but not alone, sipping spruce tea and speaking in low tones to one of the older packers. Spread throughout the group were the other red jacketed Constables of the White Pass outpost.

Grant entered with Strickland and was met with respectful nods and lifted cups. He shed his coat and gloves and slid into a narrow space at the table's end. A Constable placed a heavy bowl of stew in front of him, thick with potato, onion, salt pork, and a mystery meat that smelled better than it looked. A torn heel of bread followed, warm and dense.

Strickland stood at the head of the room and raised his tin mug. "To the men who brought the post. To the road behind, and the trail ahead."

Walters stood and followed suit. "To the ones you lost."

Grant stood and offered a simple addition, "To new friends."

"Hear, hear," Strickland answered.

Tin mugs clinked. Quiet voices echoed with shared gravity. The sound of spoons scraping wood bowls resumed, accompanied by the occasional clatter of boots or the rustle of a horse blanket being aired near the stove.

Conversations ebbed and flowed, stories of close calls on the trail, of frozen boots and buckled saddles, of tricks learned from George and quiet encouragements passed along over a campfire's fading coals at dawn. Even the packers contributed, speaking softly in accented English or in Tlingit, offering observations that needed no explanation or exaggeration.

At one point, Walters leaned across to Grant and said, "Did you ever think we'd walk out of that valley intact?"

Grant smiled faintly. "We didn't walk out. We clawed our way out."

George, overhearing, nodded once. "Claws work. Teeth too."

Laughter followed. Honest, low, and short-lived, but real. It wasn't a feast, it was a celebration. For this small, brief moment the border station at White Pass felt like more than a frozen outpost. It felt like a place where something hard had been earned by them all.

They had brought the mail. And with it, something heavier than letters: proof that the wild could be crossed, if not tamed, because of belief and determination. The lines between soldier and scout, Mountie and packer, all blurred under the shared roof.

Grant shared a few words with Walters about the descent, and they spoke briefly of the ambush, how close it had come to falling apart. George nodded once at their recollection, then simply said, "We were never alone. The trail chose us to survive."

Later, as second helpings were offered and more tea was poured, someone passed around a flask, and it made a slow circle through discreet hands. No one drank deeply, not here, but each sip carried its own shared meaning: for survival, for unity, for the road to come.

Later, when the stove's fire was low and the cold crept back in, Grant stepped outside and looked up at the stars. The wind had calmed. Behind them, the trail was dark and unforgiving. Ahead, Bennett and the end of this mission waited for him.

For tonight, Grant allowed himself a smile, because he had won. He had made it back home against all odds because he believed it could be done. He had been helped along the way, and he was grateful for the journey and the people who had brought him here.

CHAPTER XXVI

Farewells & Descents

The summit camp was already stirring long before the dawn broke its way through the clouds. Whisps of smoke from breakfast fires wound their way upwards through the rarity that was still air. The storm that had haunted their approach had blown itself out overnight, leaving the mountains clear and bright in the morning light. Crystals of ice clung to the eaves, catching the light in sharp fragments.

Grant was awake early, already dressed, the edges of fatigue still hanging on him like the dust of the trail. He stepped outside of the tent that had sheltered him through the night to survey the frozen silence. As his boots crunched over the packed snow, he found Sergeant Walters near the stables. He was tightening the straps around the bedroll on his bundled rucksack. The Buffalo Soldiers had marched up the mountains and they would march back to the coast the same way.

Seeing Grant approaching, Walters adjusted his gloves as he asked, “You headed out today?”

Grant nodded. “Down the trail, headed on to Bennett.”

“A mass exodus,” Walters joked.

“Just another day at White Pass,” Grant replied. “The traffic rarely lingers here. You’re heading back to Skagway?”

“We’ll get back and then move our camp over to Dyea.”

“To enjoy some peace and quiet?”

“I doubt that. This is the wrong profession to go looking for some peace and quiet.”

Grant extended a hand. “Couldn’t have pulled this off without you Yankees.”

Walters gripped it firmly and replied, "You Canadians are a special breed. An endangered one. It only felt right to make sure you got home in one piece."

"We'll meet again, I suspect."

"Down the trail?"

"Down the trail."

Private Hill came up behind Walters with his own rucksack slung over one shoulder. "Sir," he said to Grant, offering a tight smile. "Never thought I'd be eating stew in Canada a week ago. Glad I could make this trip."

Grant chuckled. "I'm glad you made it as well."

Private Baker followed, his arm still wrapped tight from a bruising fall a few days earlier. "Never been so cold in my life, Constable. But it felt like I was doing something that mattered. Thank you for that."

"No, I must thank all of you. You saved my bacon."

"Hell, I think you woulda killed all of them men without us," Hill chimed in.

"Private..." the long-suffering Walters groaned.

"What? Grant knows. He knows."

"Thank you, Private Hill." Grant said, well pleased.

"Shit, you're welcome." Hill replied and shouldered his pack.

"We going any time soon, Sergeant? The mountain ain't gonna get unclimbed all by itself."

"You see what I'm dealing with?" Walter asked Grant. Nodding his head towards Hill, he added, "on second thought, take me with you."

"Anytime," Grant replied with a laugh. "Anytime."

A few more laughs were shared as the other Buffalo Soldiers geared up. Words fell away, replaced by the kind of silence forged only on by shared experience. With the similar level of fanfare that their departure from Skagway had merited, they shared a wave and a nod of the head as they marched away from the outpost. Once the group had crossed back over the border, it was only a short passage of time before they crested the first ridge of their descent and disappeared. Grant had remained the entire time, watching them recede back into their own country.

Back at the Log Cabin, Grant found Strickland poring over reports and manifests.

"They've crossed back over," Grant said.

Strickland nodded. "Good men."

"They didn't have to come."

"No, but they did all the same," observed Strickland as he closed his ledger and stood. "Sometimes, that's the difference that matters most."

As they walked together through the camp, the sounds of a functioning outpost rose around them: the ring of a hammer, the rattle of a stove lid, the snort of pack animals being watered. The smell of boiled coffee, fresh-sawn pine and wood smoke cut through the cold air.

Strickland adjusted his gloves and glanced sidelong at Grant. "We'll need more hands. More eyes in more places across the Klondike. That railway will drag the world north faster than we'll be ready."

"And not just the honest world," Grant said.

Strickland stopped beside a crate and tapped it lightly. "We can't touch Smith. As much as you want to take him down, it'll never be us, not directly. He's American trouble on American soil. Skagway isn't ours to police."

"But he's reaching here," Grant replied. "We're still cleaning up the damage he's caused, the lives he's ruined."

They stood in silence a moment, watching a young constable string a clothesline between two supply tents, his fingers clumsy from the cold.

"You're not wrong. However, the Klondike has enough devils of its own," Strickland said. "We've got murders in Dawson, theft in Bennett, claims being jumped every week, and half the territory running on whiskey and rumour. We can't afford to chase shadows across borders."

"I hear you. I'll ride on to Bennett," Grant said. "Jorge will be waiting. Steele, too. We'll finish what we started."

Strickland gave a long nod. "You're the right man for it. You proved that."

Grant hesitated. "Thompson should've been here for it."

"He knew the risk. We all did. Doesn't make it hurt any less."

Grant swallowed and looked toward a distant ridgeline. "I keep hearing his voice. Just before the ambush. He was joking about his boots. Said he'd trade a gold claim for some dry socks."

"Then carry that," Strickland said. "His voice. We all carry someone. It'll be up to you to decide if that becomes a heavy weight, or a light one. Joy is an easier load to bear, I've found. If light can speak to you in darkness, then you'll never be alone."

Grant nodded once more, then turned. "I'll take your point. Time for me to saddle up."

Strickland didn't stop him. He merely said, "Ride safe. When you see Steele, give him this." Strickland held up a sealed envelope. Tell him the post has come through."

Grant allowed himself the smallest of smiles. As they turned back toward the cluster of tents and wind-lashed buildings, the snow crunching underfoot like dry parchment. There was more work ahead. There always was. The frontier wasn't something you bent to rule. It had to be respected; and that respect had to be earned to understand it. One frozen outpost or one hard-won mile at a time.

Heading toward the stables, a fresh wind gust tore its way through the pass. Grant paused, his eyes narrowing toward the southern ridges. Far in the distance, a thin curl of smoke spiralled upward, faint against the bright sky.

"Still watching," Strickland muttered.

Grant didn't reply immediately. He stared into the horizon, into the place where the trail vanished beyond the fold of trees and snowfields.

"Soapy's men?"

"Could be. Could be anything or anyone." Strickland's jaw tightened. "Whoever it is, they're waiting to see what we'll do next. They're waiting to find a gap."

Grant exhaled through his nose, the breath white and sharp. "Then let's not give them one and then take it away just as quick."

For Strickland, the traffic was still headed his way. For Grant, the trail wasn't finished with him. Not yet.

CHAPTER XXVII

The Return to Bennett

At the front of the reduced convoy's column, Grant sat in his saddle with a battered slouch and a satisfied look on his face. Mud-caked well past its knees, the black mare under him was trailing the scent of sweat and pine. Behind him came George, impassive and steady as always, followed by the four packers leading their train of eight horses heavily laden with battered canvas baggage.

Despite being back in Canada, their pace had been steady and cautious. Their approach to Bennett was quiet. The Dead Horse Trail and White Pass lay behind them, but its toll was etched into every boot, every cracked saddle, every unread letter now safely tucked into the stacked canvas dunnage bags they carried. The trail had finally eased, and the worst was behind them. The land around them bloomed with spring and buzzed with the rising tide of insect life. The wind had died off and the infuriating hordes of blackflies clouded around the faces of the men and horses alike.

When they reached the first clearing overlooking the lake, the town came into view: a squat cluster of buildings and tents hugging the shoreline. The town had shrunk significantly since Grant had left. The bulk of its population had been entirely transient. Once their boats were built, tents had come down and they were off again, pushing further north. Lake Bennett stretched out ahead of them, wide, blue and ice-free. Its waters flat with the complete absence of wind. Dozens of those small, hastily built boats were seen cutting across it: scows, canoes, patched steamers, squat barges, all being paddled with an inefficient frenzy and headed towards an unlikely future on the Yukon River.

Grant looked towards the NWMP detachment. Stood apart from the chaotic jumble of the townsite, it was all squared timbers, order and red coats among the sea of canvas and ambition. Something was different though, a red flag hung limp on the crooked pole over the detachment. Grant noticed it at once but was unable to make out any further detail. He pulled his horse to a slow halt at the crest of the trail and stared towards the flaccid new flag.

"That's not the Union Jack," he muttered aloud. "Red Ensign?"

George, riding behind him, said nothing. The four Tlingit packers fanned out behind them, their packhorses still trudging, their breath visible in the early June air.

Making their way through the settlement, Bennett was slumped over like an exhausted runner: abandoned patchwork wooden shanties were listing on the thawed ground, stained tents that had been abandoned were bowed and lay damp across puddles, the narrow outpost roads were carved with ruts deep enough to swallow even a horse. Men shouted from docks. Women boiled laundry over campfires on the shoreline. Filthy children chased stray dogs through the muck. Bennett was alive, no longer swollen, but it still rippled with the movement and noise of human endeavour.

Entering the detachment's main yard, Grant lead the way in towards the rudimentary stables. Nearby, Sergeant Flynn stood straighter when he saw the convoy enter, his eyes scanned each man, noting every step, every breath.

"Well, I'll be damned," he said. "Didn't think I'd see you again, Grant."

Grant dismounted, his boots hitting thawed earth. The red ensign caught his eye again. He nodded towards it, "Afternoon Sergeant. When did we start flying that?"

"Inspector Steele's orders," Flynn replied. "He said it was time we marked ourselves differently. We're not just British subjects: we're the Dominion of Canada after all."

Grant looked up once more. A gust of wind snatched at its corners. "It looks good to me," he said.

Flynn stared at him for a long moment. His face was unreadable, but his hands were steady. He asked, “Still breathing, then?”

“Not for lack of those trying otherwise,” Grant replied.

“You and that trail have a habit of surviving each other. That’ll run out someday.”

Grant gave a tired smile. “Not today.”

Flynn approached, his voice quieter now. “I said some things. When last we saw each other.”

“I know.”

Flynn met his eyes. “I was wrong. Despite everything, even after Dorsey was arrested, I still suspected you were bent and part of the whole McCade conspiracy.”

Grant thought back on Sergeant Dorsey, the former Quartermaster at White Pass who had been on the take from McCade and his gang. Dorsey had tried to distract the detachment and prevent reinforcements from assisting White Pass from McCade’s attack by claiming Grant was the mastermind behind the gang.

Grant snorted and observed, “As I recall, there were a couple more curses were attached to my being ‘bent’.”

“True,” Flynn agreed. “After hearing about the ambush on the Chilkoot? It was made very clear to me that you didn’t deserve my distrust. I apologize. Mea culpa, they say.”

“Let’s move past it, Sergeant. Soapy Smith’s goons like to play games and sow discord however they can.”

“I appreciate that,” Sergeant Flynn said and offered his hand in peace.

Grant nodded and shook the hand firmly, “How about you help us unload all of this post?”

Flynn rounded up some of the other Constables and they all helped unload the horses together. The Tlingit packers moved quietly, unloading the sealed sacks and laying them with care against the far wall of the palisade. The scent of pine tar, sweat, and horse clung to everything in the still air.

“We’ll have to rig some sort of sail or temporary tenting to keep the elements off it,” Grant suggested to Sergeant Flynn.

"We'll go round up some of the discarded tents around town," Flynn replied. "You wouldn't believe what has simply been left behind."

Jorge's column appeared at the gates of the detachment not long after the last bag had been unloaded. His face split into a grin when he saw Grant.

"You made it, cabrón!"

"So did you."

Jorge grunted as he slid down from his horse, mud caked up to his waist, his hat crushed into a shape only loosely resembling its original form. He clapped a hand against Grant's shoulder. "Don't tell me everything. Just tell me it's over."

"Until people stop writing letters," Grant replied. "I think we'll continue to have our hands full."

"Good luck with that," Jorge quipped. "I meant with you and that Soapy."

"I know. He's a problem. But he's not ours. Unless our paths cross again, I'm done with him."

"That's good to hear," Jorge sighed with relief.

Summoned by a rider, Sam Steele arrived within the hour. He entered the detachment's yard with the calm presence of a man who had long learned to keep his emotions sheathed. His coat was dusted with thick globs of mud, but his eyes were bright.

"Constable Grant," Steele said, extending his hand. "You've done something most men wouldn't even attempt."

"We did it as a unit, Superintendent." Grant replied and indicated towards Jorge, George and the respective teams of packers still busy stacking the canvas wrapped baggage layer by layer, underneath the tents that Flynn and the other Constables were rigging. "I could never had done this alone. We brought every letter we could carry. Including this one from Inspector Strickland."

Grant removed the sealed letter from his uniform jacket and offered it to his superior.

Steele accepted the letter and said, "I'll read this and then we'll speak further. Report to my office after you've finished out here."

A few hours later, Grant was seated in Steele's tiny office at the rear of the barracks.

"I read the preliminary report," Steele said. "Tell me what this piece of paper doesn't."

Grant told him. Of the trail. Of the ambushes, the standoff with Soapy's advance men. Of Jorge's qualities. Of George's quiet vigilance. Of Soapy's insufferable resolve. Of the loss of Thompson and Young. Steele listened, hands clasped on the desk before him. When Grant finished, Steele gave a slow nod at the end. "You gave this territory something rare. A taste of certainty."

"I'm not so sure about that," Grant opined. "I got lucky."

"You crossed the trail with a skeleton crew, a pair, rather, of skeleton crews and with every odd stacked against you. That's not luck. That's leadership. For starters, I'm promoting you Corporal." Steele pushed back from the desk and gestured towards the door. "Walk with me."

It was neither a request nor an order. The Superintendent made his statement feel more like a conversation between equals, rather than a duty to a superior.

As Steele and Grant left the office, they made their way through the barracks and out into the main yard.

"All of our detachments are sending men here to collect the post and distribute it around the region. I'll speak with your man George and with Jorge. Hopefully they'll stay on, if they're willing."

Grant nodded. "We'll need to rotate patrols. Schedule mail runs. Pair our men with locals who know the terrain like George."

"Agreed. We'll find fresh men and rotate teams in and out. For the next while, you'll help lay the foundation of that and anchor the process. After that, I want you in Dawson."

"I'll be happy to go north, sir."

"Good. It's where the challenges are. More gold or less gold, it does not matter. There are more people up there. No food. More problems. There's all the temptation and we cannot let anyone like a Soapy Smith get their talons hooked into it. The opportunity to cut corners, to bribe their way into matters and then twist and pervert justice? That, I shall not tolerate. I want lawmen up there who know what I want. Who I trust."

"You think I'm that man?"

"I know you are Corporal Grant. The Klondike's changing faster than we are. We either keep up, or we will get swept aside."

"We'll hold it," Grant said. "We have to."

The wind came up quickly and cut across the lake like a knife. The Red Ensign of the Dominion of Canada unfurled out and snapped to attention, flapping taut against the new gusts to reveal its full majesty.

The outpost below it, like the promise of peace, order and good government which the ensign stood for, would hold fast against the wilds. Come morning, the North-West Mounted Police's work would begin yet again.

CHAPTER XXVIII

Juneau Wharf

That July day, Skagway had stank of rain and restlessness.

By noon, the clouds had dropped to street level, turning the town into a smear of soot and fog. The boardwalks gleamed slick with drizzle. Gutters overflowed and the streets filled with runoff from the mountains, carrying filth and bits of torn paper down into the bay.

Inside the saloons, the tension was rowdy. The laughter was becoming too loud and the piano keys struck too hard. Outside, the streets pulsed with something quieter, meaner. Word had spread: Soapy Smith had pulled yet another scam, and this time he'd crossed the wrong man. Twenty-eight hundred in raw Yukon gold had been conned out of a Klondiker fresh off the trail. An earnest boy no older than twenty with red hands and a trembling voice who had been too trusting and too green to know any better than bet on one of Soapy's rigged three card Monte games. The boy's gold had vanished into Smith's empire of crooked smiles and quick hands.

The town wasn't just angry, it was shifting. It had hit its limit and was bleeding resentment.

The Committee of 101, an informal association of vigilantes who were sick of the law's inability or incapability to resist the Soap Gang, had called for a gathering. It was unofficial, but they were clear. No posters, no loud proclamations. It was a whisper that grew into a murmur, one that drifted through every store, bunkhouse and back alley. By the early evening, the docks were full. The fog clung low over the water, thick and greasy. Lanterns swung from iron hooks, painting dim shadows across the salt-worn planks. Merchants, miners, barkeeps, gamblers, freight haulers, and a few off-duty U.S. soldiers stood packed together beneath the slate sky. None spoke as they waited for the meeting to begin. A cough here, a boot scrape there. It was the kind of silence that warned of a fully brewed storm, one that was simmering until its moment came.

No Mounties were present. Not today. This wasn't a Canadian matter, but the red coated lawmen had recently shown the town it was possible to stand up to a problem. In this case: to their bully. This was Skagway's reckoning.

Six blocks away, the doors of Jeff Smith's Parlor banged open. Soapy Smith staggered outside, drunk and determined, a man stepping out into a world he believed owed him a favour. The usually immaculate gangster's long black coat was unbuttoned, his shirt was askew, his cravat hung loose. He had a Winchester cradled casually across the crook of his arm. His sneering face was flushed with drink. His eyes were glassy but dangerous.

Later, it was said that he had been furious, raging and slamming bottles into the Parlor's walls when he had heard the news. A meeting? Without him? He wasn't just offended, he was enraged. Texas Jack was not there to cool him down. When told there was trouble brewing at the docks, he had been heard to yell in reply, "By God, trouble is what I am looking for!"

With several of his goons following a short distance behind him, the Winchester toting Soapy strode through the town towards the docks. When he arrived, the sea wind dragged at his coat and his boots thumped across the wharf's planks.

"You boys wait here," Soapy ordered his entourage as swung the rifle over his shoulder and walked swiftly onto Juneau Wharf. "I'll talk these yahoos down from their high horse."

Approaching a pair of men, Soapy waved his hand at them, shooing them away like barflies. "The pair of ya! Outta my way. Get off this damn wharf."

The two men jumped the rail to the sand six feet below to avoid Smith's fury. As he continued to make his way towards the meeting, another pair of men, both hired as security guards turned to face Smith. The oncoming gangster did not even acknowledge them. He breezed right past their lack of resistance.

However, this was seen by another man. He had been hired to guard the meeting and keep the Soap Gang away. Frank Reid, a man who lived up to his word, stepped forwards. He held up his hand. He was lean, wind-cut, and stone-faced. An engineer by trade, a veteran by experience. He wore no uniform, no badge, just a canvas coat, a .38 revolver tucked into his waistband and the quiet authority of a strong man tired of watching good people get stomped on.

"You're not going down there Soapy," Reid said, blocking the other man's path.

"Evening Frank," Soapy called out, stopping ten paces away. "Didn't peg you for a joiner."

"Put the rifle down, Soapy. It ends here."

Soapy squinted at Reid. As he slowed, he continued his approach and asked, "Are you threatening me?"

"The town's done with you. They're done with being afraid."

Soapy smiled. It wasn't his charming smile. It was the other one. The one that preceded sending more than one man to their grave. "The town's done when I say it's done. I'll tell the town what they need."

Reid's hand rested on the grip of the revolver in the waistband of his trousers. "Maybe once. Not anymore."

"You planning on giving me the rope, Frank?" Soapy challenged him in return. "Not likely."

"You're not taking another step towards this meeting," Reid warned him.

Soapy didn't stop walking and replied, "Like hell I'm not."

When Soapy's rifle swung off his shoulder, Reid moved. Guns barked. Two shots were followed by silence.

Then came another shot.

Reid staggered, blood blooming across his side. But Soapy dropped dead to the wharf, struck square in the chest. The Winchester clattered as it hit the planks hard. His boots twitching, blood spilled out under his body like ink in a rainstorm. The wind caught the brim of his hat and sent it tumbling into the harbour.

No one moved.

Reid slumped against a piling, clutching his side. "Someone... see to him," he gasped. "Someone see that it's over."

It was.

Witnesses would later disagree on what had happened. What is certain: Soapy had swung his Winchester around and Reid reached for his pistol. Both men fired.

Reid was shot through the groin and abdomen, wounds that would prove fatal twelve days later. He managed to get a shot off, grazing Soapy's arm. The final blow had come when young Jesse Murphy, one of the committee's guards Soapy had breezed past earlier, wrestled the rifle away and turned it back on its owner. He fired once.

Soapy Smith was struck in the heart and died before his body fell. Pandemonium followed. Murphy dropped the rifle and like others, fled into the fog. Others rushed to Reid's side. Someone called out for a doctor, but even then, everyone, including Frank, knew it looked to be a bad outcome.

Soapy was carried back to the Parlor by his few remaining men. His body was washed, laid out, and quietly buried the next day in the local cemetery. There was no parade. No defiance. Just a short service in the church he had once helped to fund. The minister, stone-faced, in his sermon, read from Proverbs 13, "The way of transgressors is hard."

Twelve days later, Frank Reid succumbed to gangrene. The town mourned him as a hero. A monument would rise in his name, chiselled from stone and resolve.

Skagway began to shift. Soapy's empire, the con games, fake telegraphs and bribed deputies fell apart almost overnight. The gamblers and grifters moved on. The town started over.

From the door of the warehouse filling yet again with fresh post from around the world, Staff Sergeant Hyles watched the town in silence. He had seen how quick lawlessness could rot the bones of a place. But the renewal and healing that had come in the wake of Soapy's death was momentous. This was something else, Skagway had leached itself of its own poison.

Hyles lit his pipe. After shaking out the match, he stared out toward the harbour. The summer mists were rolling in again, thick and uncertain. "It's over," he said quietly to himself.

But, the Klondike's wind whispered back: not yet.
The frontier never really sleeps. It only changes its face.

Manufactured by Amazon.ca
Bolton, ON

55870539R00113